JIT FORECASTING AND MASTER SCHEDULING
Not an Oxymoron

By J. David Viale

A FIFTY-MINUTE™ SERIES BOOK

CRISP PUBLICATIONS, INC.
Menlo Park, California

JIT FORECASTING AND MASTER SCHEDULING
Not an Oxymoron

J. David Viale

CREDITS
Managing Editor: **Kathleen Barcos**
Editor: **Chris Carrigan**
Production: **Leslie Power**
Typesetting: **ExecuStaff**
Cover Design: **Daniel Burney**

All rights reserved. No part of this book may be reproduced or transmitted in any form or by any means now known or to be invented, electronic or mechanical, including photocopying, recording, or by any information storage or retrieval system without written permission from the author or publisher, except for the brief inclusion of quotations in a review.

Copyright © 1996 by J. David Viale Jr.
Printed in the United States of America by Bawden Printing Company.

> Distribution to the U.S. Trade:
> National Book Network, Inc.
> 4720 Boston Way
> Lanham, MD 20706
> 1-800-462-6420

Library of Congress Catalog Card Number 96-72501
Viale, J. David
JIT Forecasting and Master Scheduling
ISBN 1-56052-424-3

10 9 8 7 6 5 4 3 2 1

This book is printed on recyclable paper with soy ink.

LEARNING OBJECTIVES FOR:

JIT FORECASTING AND MASTER SCHEDULING

The objectives for *JIT Forecasting and Master Scheduling* are listed below. They have been developed to guide you, the reader, to the core issues covered in this book.

Objectives

- ❏ 1) to explain the techniques and advantages of long-term planning.

- ❏ 2) to present a just-in-time forecasting model.

- ❏ 3) to explain how to use forecasting tools.

Assessing Your Progress

In addition to the Learning Objectives, *JIT Forecasting and Master Scheduling* includes a unique new **assessment tool*** which can be found at the back of this book. A twenty-five item, multiple choice/true-false questionnaire allows the reader to evaluate his or her comprehension of the subject matter covered. An answer sheet, with a chart matching the questions to the listed objectives, is also provided.

* Assessments should not be used in any selection process.

ABOUT THE AUTHOR

J. David Viale is the founder and president of the Center for Manufacturing Education, an international education and training company.

Dave's career in education started as a high-school teacher, then he went on to teach at various colleges and universities.

His background includes management positions at Arthur Andersen, Hewlett-Packard and Fairchild Semiconductor. He was a practicing CPA and is certified in production and inventory management (CPIM).

His diverse business and teaching background gives him a unique blend of theory, practicality and financial impact. With this diverse experience, he brings a cross-functional perspective to his classes, speeches, seminars and key executive presentations, which he delivers across the United States, Canada, Europe and the Far East.

He can be contacted at:

>   Phone: 408-973-0309
>   Fax: 408-973-1592

ABOUT THE SERIES

With over 200 titles in print, the acclaimed Crisp 50-Minute™ series presents self-paced learning at its easiest and best. These comprehensive self-study books for business or personal use are filled with exercises, activities, assessments, and case studies that capture your interest and increase your understanding.

Other Crisp products, based on the 50-Minute books, are available in a variety of learning style formats for both individual and group study, including audio, video, CD-ROM, and computer-based training.

CONTENTS

INTRODUCTION vii

MODULE I   TODAY'S KEY COMPETITIVE CHALLENGES 1
   Today's Business Challenges 3
   Industry's Top Seven Competitive Issues 4

**MODULE II   LONG-TERM PLANNING: THE KEYS TO JIT
               FORECASTING AND MASTER SCHEDULING** 13
   Business Planning 15
   Environments and Their Effects on Inventory Management 19
   Production and Resource Planning 21
   Balancing the Imbalances 25
   Conflicting Goals of Strategic Planning 27

MODULE III   JIT FORECASTING: THE MODEL 39
   Forecasted Sales 41
   JIT Forecasting Objectives 42
   The Forecasting Model 44
   Forecast Error 46
   Five Steps to a JIT Forecasting Model 48

MODULE IV   JIT FORECASTING: THE TOOLS 53
   Forecasting Tools 55
   Using Intrinsic Forecasting Tools 59
   Using Extrinsic Forecasting Tools 67
   Forecasting Methods 68
   The Key to JIT Forecasting 69
   The 80/20 Rule 76

MODULE V   JIT MASTER SCHEDULING 93
   Why JIT Master Scheduling? 95
   Steps to Developing the Master Schedule 96

ASSESSMENT 117

INTRODUCTION

The world of business is changing rapidly and dramatically. No longer do we see the stability of the past; constant reorganization is becoming the standard. Business organizations are having to reinvent themselves continuously to meet the demands of a global marketplace.

Companies throughout the world face the challenge of developing the most highly-educated and diverse workforce ever known. Because requirements for skill-levels continue to increase, less educated workers are struggling to find jobs. The competition for skilled workers will only become more intense.

This book is intended for people entering the field of manufacturing, for those employed in functional areas such as manufacturing, sales, marketing, finance, human resources, research and development and who wish to develop a fundamental knowledge of how forecasting and master scheduling works.

The information contained herein will be invaluable to your organization when customers ask you to:

- Achieve faster turnaround times.

- Carry their inventory at no charge.

- Be flexible. React to change with no increase in cost.

More important, this book challenges you to upgrade your existing skills and acquire new ones. Regardless of your present skill level, you have the opportunity to increase your knowledge of JIT Forecasting and Master Scheduling. No matter how process-oriented your organization is, there is always room for improvement. By using the information and tools presented in this book, you will

- ▶ Acquire a fundamental understanding of various interrelations and responsibilities in the manufacturing environments as they relate to JIT forecasting, master scheduling, and inventory levels.

- ▶ Acquire a knowledge of common manufacturing terms.

INTRODUCTION (continued)

- ▶ Recognize potential conflicts among these areas. Although you may not have the expertise in each area to resolve differences or make decisions, you will know what key choices must be made in working out solutions.

- ▶ Develop a business perspective of business planning, production planning, forecasting, master scheduling, and inventory setting.

- ▶ Have a tested model for improving forecasting and master scheduling.

Think of every day as a page in the résumé of your life. Ask yourself, "What am I doing every day to increase my net worth, to make myself more marketable?" This book supports you in taking control of your own learning process, by continuously improving.

> "The Continuous Improvement Process is not only a way of doing business; it's a way of doing life—the essence of lifelong learning."
> —J. David Viale

MODULE I

Today's Key Competitive Challenges

Learning Objectives

After completing this module, you will be able to:

- Determine major challenges facing business

- List industry's top seven needs

- Describe why JIT Forecasting is the missing link in the customer-supplier chain

TODAY'S BUSINESS CHALLENGES

Business today is under pressure to create high-quality products, deliver products to market faster, reduce costs, increase flexibility by reacting to change, and improve its workforce continually through training and education. Organizations that want to stay competitive and make a profit must accomplish these objectives. Forecasting and master scheduling play key roles in meeting these challenges. Let's go over the top seven competitive issues facing industry today.

Industry's Top Seven Competitive Issues

#1 Improve Forecasting Accuracy

#2 Bring Products to Market Faster

#3 Reduce Costs

#4 Deliver High-Quality Products Through Continuous Improvement

#5 Make Changes Faster and More Manageable

#6 Improve Employee Training and Education

#7 Improve Information Systems and Networks

INDUSTRY'S TOP SEVEN COMPETITIVE ISSUES

#1 Improve Forecasting Accuracy

The major causes of poor customer-service performance in terms of on-time delivery are inaccurate customer forecasts, a multitude of changes to the original customer orders, and an overall lack of account management—not suppliers, not purchasing. The result is excessive inventory, which can ultimately lead to inventory write-offs and high product cost and lower profit margins.

The more accurate the individual product-sales forecasting is, the smaller the forecast error, and the less inventory needs to be carried to maintain a specified level of customer service. By carrying less inventory, the capacity of machines required to build products is better utilized. Inventory is not built before it is needed, thus avoiding the mistake of committing capacity of machines too early. By carrying less inventory, less space is used, and it is not used or paid for before it is needed.

A basic premise of this book states that, *"the larger the forecast error, the higher the desired customer service level, the more inventory that must be carried."* And we are not talking about inventory at the supplier, unless there is willingness to pay expenses such as storage, insurance, and other related carrying costs. These costs are some of the major "hidden costs of manufacturing" contributing to the fact that many companies have increasing revenues and decreasing profits (and stock prices).

The solution to managing these costs is the establishment of a JIT forecasting and master scheduling model that will be discussed throughout this book.

Historically, Just-in-Time principles have focused only on JIT production and JIT purchasing. However, when forecasts fluctuate as they all do, inventories start to pile up in finished goods, work-in-process (WIP), raw materials, and in the inventories of suppliers. This has a real impact on the JIT program. The objective of this book is to develop a module for JIT forecasting and master scheduling to help reduce the forecast error and the inventory levels, and support the total JIT program. To prove that JIT Forecasting and Master Scheduling is not an oxymoron.

#2 Bring Products to Market Faster

Products are coming to market faster and faster, and the time to recoup the investment is getting shorter because the life cycle of each succeeding product decreases. When you reduce the amount of time it takes to get each new product to market, you have less time in which to earn profit. As a result, products must be profitable sooner so that the next generation of new products can be funded.

The typical Product Life Cycle (introduction, growth, maturity, decline, and demise) shown in Figure 1-1 demonstrates some of the issues of shorter life cycles.

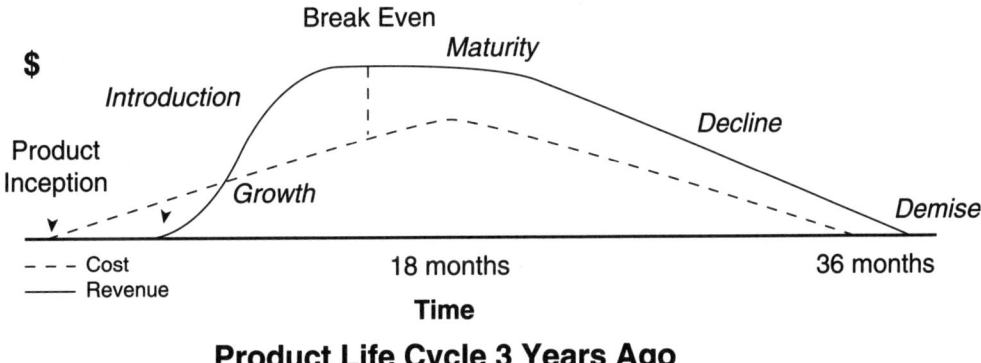

Product Life Cycle 3 Years Ago

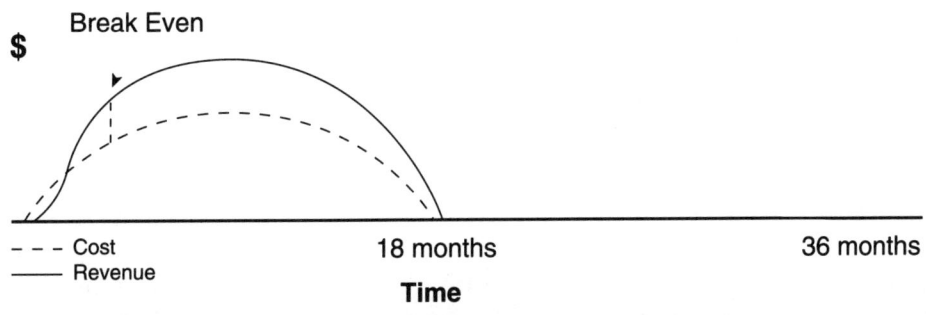

Product Life Cycle Today (18 months or less)

Figure 1-1: Product Life Cycle

INDUSTRY'S TOP SEVEN COMPETITIVE ISSUES (continued)

The impact, if nothing is done to reduce cost significantly, is potentially devastating to the profitability over a product's lifetime. Companies are grappling with ways to change the slope of the revenue curve (up and to the left) and of the cost curve (down and to the right) by gauging success based on new measures including:

▶ **TIME TO MARKET:** How fast can you get the product to market?

▶ **TIME TO VOLUME:** How fast can you produce at a volume that attracts enough revenue to cover costs?

▶ **TIME TO CONSUMPTION:** How fast does the customer make the decision to buy?

▶ **TIME TO PROFIT:** How fast can you generate revenue that exceeds cost?

▶ **TIME TO CHANGE:** How fast can you make changes to accommodate customer requests and how much does the change affect your profit? Reducing the number of changes to the product (Engineering Change Orders) as early in the new product development cycle as possible.

In this book we show you how improvements in forecasting, master scheduling, just-in-time manufacturing, inventory management and other areas respond to all of these challenges.

#3 Reduce Costs

There are many ways to reduce costs. Profits grow when you decrease costs, increase revenue, or a combination of both. Consider the following example of cost reduction. In this example our

> Unit sales price is: $10.00
> Profit margin % is: 10%
> Profit margin is: $1.00

If we were to decrease any cost by $1.00, the profit in this case would double. Another way of looking at this is: $1.00 in cost reduction is equal to $10 in sales.

To maximize profits, your organization needs to reduce both tangible and intangible costs. This can be done by:

- Reducing the amount of time inventory spends under the company's ownership. This enables you to reduce other costs, such as rental space, insurance to cover inventory, interest on money borrowed to pay for inventory, or computed interest on money that could have been earned. By reducing inventory and selling it faster, you improve cash flow.

- Reducing the number of decisions that must be made to introduce a new product, as well as the number of authorizations needed once a decision has been made.

- Reducing defects and variability in processes.

- Reducing wasted time. Intangible costs are the biggest component of getting product to the customer faster. Time is wasted by unproductive meetings, telephone tag, and interruptions. More time frees you to be more productive and make more decisions.

By applying the simple techniques presented in this book, you can achieve cost reductions and improve your company's profitability.

#4 Deliver High-Quality Products Through Continuous Improvement

Organizations need or exceed customer expectations with regard to quality. The driving force behind quality improvement is the need to bring a quality product to market faster. The idea is to improve quality on an ongoing basis. When every process continually improves, quality improves, costs go down, profits go up, and new products reach the market more quickly.

INDUSTRY'S TOP SEVEN COMPETITIVE ISSUES (continued)

#5 Make Changes Faster and More Manageable

The organizations that are best at managing change have the competitive advantage. Customers ask for faster turnaround times or other changes. You must be able to input these changes, analyze the changes and their consequences, then make decisions. You will never be able to control change, but you can manage it. Change is manageable if your organization can anticipate and respond to change.

#6 Improve Employee Training and Education

To increase your organization's ability to respond to change, your employees need to be trained and educated in manufacturing theory, business and financial issues, and continuous process improvement. Customers will expand their purchases based not only on your products and processes, but also on your employees' education and training at all levels. Ask yourself, "What person in my organization or department would I **least** like our customers to talk to in terms of understanding our quality processes?"

Executives at all levels in organizations may have spent significant money educating their people. Unfortunately, the executives themselves often have not remained current. As a result, many find themselves making decisions about issues of which they have little or no understanding.

A major responsibility of everyone in your organization is to educate everyone else. Education and training may be the ultimate competitive weapon a company has.

#7 Improve Information Systems and Networks

Information systems are the new bottleneck. Change is happening so fast that information systems can't keep up. More advanced information systems and networks must be developed to enhance the flow of information. In order to make better decisions, you need to get information faster.

EXERCISE 1

1. List the seven challenges facing business today. (Which do you think are most important?)

   _____
   _____
   _____
   _____

2. Discuss which of these are the greatest challenges facing your company.

   _____
   _____
   _____
   _____

3. List the five major components of a product life cycle.

   _____
   _____
   _____
   _____

4. (a) Mark the key points of the product life cycle below as covered in this module.

   (b) What do we call the point at which revenue equals cost?

EXERCISE 1 (continued)

5. What are the consequences of reducing the product life cycle of 36 months to 18 to nine months?

_____
_____
_____
_____

6. What are some of the ways change can be managed in your company?

_____
_____
_____
_____

7. What is the role education and training play in your career development?

_____
_____
_____
_____

EXERCISE 1 ANSWERS

1. List the seven challenges facing business today.

   - Improving forecasting accuracy
   - Bring products to market faster
   - Reduce costs
   - Deliver high-quality products through continuous improvement
   - Make changes faster and more manageable
   - Improve employee training and education
   - Improve information systems and networks

2. Discuss which of these are the greatest challenges facing your company. (Open discussion)

3. List the five major components of a product life cycle.

   - Introduction
   - Growth
   - Maturity
   - Decline
   - Demise

4. (a) Identify the key points of the product life cycle depicted below. (Open discussion)

   (b) What do we call the point at which revenue equals cost? *Break even*

5. What are the consequences of reducing the product life cycle from 36 months to 18 to nine months?

   - Profit over the shorter product life cycle goes down
   - Less funds to invest in new product development
   - Less funds to fund capital acquisitions, build new facilities, pay for salaries and materials

EXERCISE 1 ANSWERS (continued)

6. What are some of the ways change can be managed in your company?

- The organizations that are best at managing change have the competitive advantage.

- Customer requests for faster turnaround times or other changes can be accommodated.

- You must be able to input these changes, analyze the changes and their consequences, then make decisions faster.

- You will never be able to control change, but you can manage it.

- Change is manageable if your organization can anticipate and respond to change.

7. What is the role education and training play in your career development?

To increase your organization's ability to respond to change, people need to be trained and educated in manufacturing theory, business and finance issues, and quality control. Customers will expand their purchases based not only on your products and processes, but also on your employees' education and training at all levels.

MODULE II

Long-Term Planning: The Keys to JIT Forecasting and Master Scheduling

Learning Objectives

After completing this module, you will be able to:

- Describe the major manufacturing environments
- Calculate a Production Plan
- Develop an outline for a Business Plan and a Manufacturing Strategy

BUSINESS PLANNING

"The best way to predict the future is to create it."

—Peter Drucker
Management Consultant

The planning process is organized by periods of time into the following general categories: long-term, medium-term and short-term. While there is disagreement as to the relative length of each category, for purposes of this book we will use the following:

Long-term planning	1 to 5 years
Medium-term planning	2 to 18 months
Short-term planning	1 to 60 days

In business, these planning periods overlap and companies will place varying degrees of emphasis on each period.

The outcomes of long-term planning activities are a business plan, a manufacturing strategy, and an annual production plan that drives the master schedule. Figure 2-1 on the next page illustrates the activities involved in long-term planning. In manufacturing circles, this big picture is called MRP II.

The planning process can be viewed as a process of checks and balances, which work in a hierarchical integrated fashion. After the business plan and related strategies have been developed, the manufacturing strategy drives the production planning process. The production plan defines volume loads by product family; the resource plan checks to make sure there are enough people, equipment and facilities, supplier capacity, and money to fund these acquisitions.

Remember, many of these expenditures are committed in anticipation of meeting forecast sales figures. This is one of the major reasons for the tremendous emphasis on month-end, quarter-end, and year-end shipments.

Any forecasting and master scheduling model must be part of an integrated planning system which spans the company's entire business planning cycle.

A **business plan** is a statement of long-range strategy supported by a projection of resources. Business plans are important in that they describe what the business looks like today, and predict what it will look like in the future. This plan sets the direction for the company. It also creates a framework in which the organization can respond to changes required to stay competitive. To give all employees a sense of where the company is headed, appropriate excerpts of the plan should be communicated to all levels of the organization; however, any competitive, sensitive information would require limited distribution.

BUSINESS PLANNING (continued)

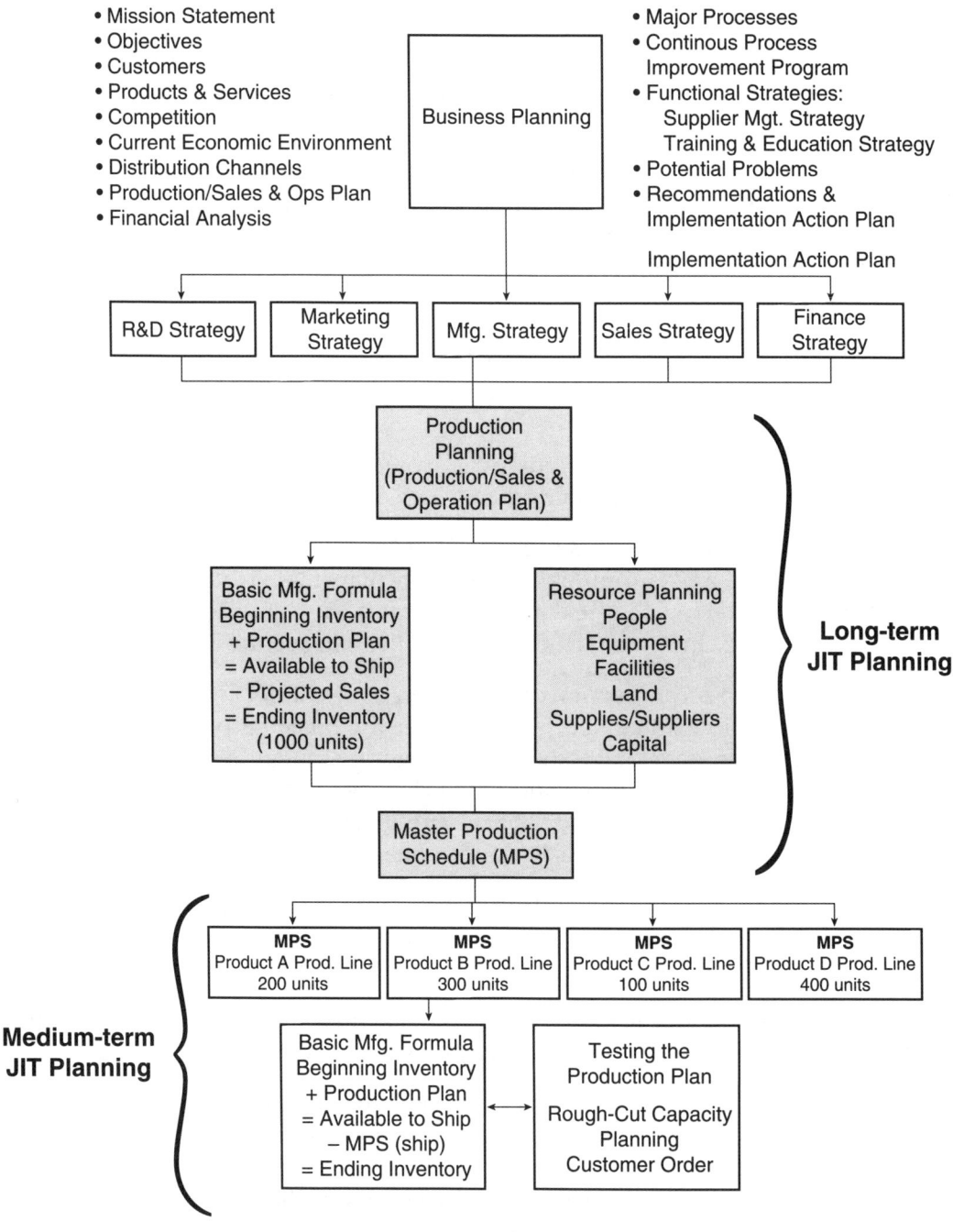

Figure 2-1: The Planning Process

COMPONENTS OF A BUSINESS PLAN

The following are components of a business plan. Some of these components are commonly found in business plans; some are not typically included but should be considered.

- Mission Statement
- Objectives
- Customers
- Products and Services
- Competition
- Current Economic and Political Environments (Environmental Scanning)
- Distribution Channels
- Production Sales and Operation Plan (including the Resource Plan)
- Financial Analysis
- Major Processes
- Continuous Process Improvement (CPI) Program
- Training and Education Strategy
- Potential Problems
- Recommendations and Implementation Plans

Business plans may be as brief as a few pages or quite lengthy. Also, business plans are meant to be updated because your business is continually changing. Developing a business plan is an iterative process, and you will need to reexamine each component and make adjustments on an ongoing basis as changes in markets, technologies, and competition take place.

Functional Strategies

A business plan should drive the different functional strategies such as R&D, Finance, Marketing, and so on. This book focuses solely on the manufacturing strategy. However, much of the discussion is applicable in other functional areas.

FORMULATE YOUR MANUFACTURING STRATEGY

The **manufacturing strategy** is one of the most important strategies because it includes the assumptions required to support the portion of the overall business plan devoted to long-term sales.

The manufacturing strategy should support the business plan and detail the following:

- Dealing with long-term market trends

- Projected growth and variability of demand

- The emergence of new technologies

- The emergence of new organization structures

- The role of information technology

- The impact of capital investment in light of shorter product life cycles

- Key competitive issues, such as time-to-market, time-to-volume, quality, costing, and managing change faster and faster

- Implementation of the JIT forecasting and master scheduling objectives to reduce the forecast error and inventory

An important component of the manufacturing strategy is a description of the plan to be used to manage each supplier. This description should answer these questions:

- What are the supplier-management objectives?

- What strategy will be used with key suppliers to ensure that supply-chain/management objectives are met?

ENVIRONMENTS AND THEIR EFFECTS ON INVENTORY MANAGEMENT

Business environments often determine the type of forecasting and master scheduling systems needed in various industries. Following is a brief overview of the major types of business environments and their impact on forecasting, master scheduling, and inventory levels.

The types of items that should be forecast might include: in a build-to-order—resource usage; in a build-to-stock—finished goods; in an assemble-to-order—options, subassemblies and common parts. Service parts, capacity of machines and other independent demands, such as end-of-life buys should also be forecasted.

The chart below illustrates that when product variety increases, the product volume decreases. The chart on the following page expands on this.

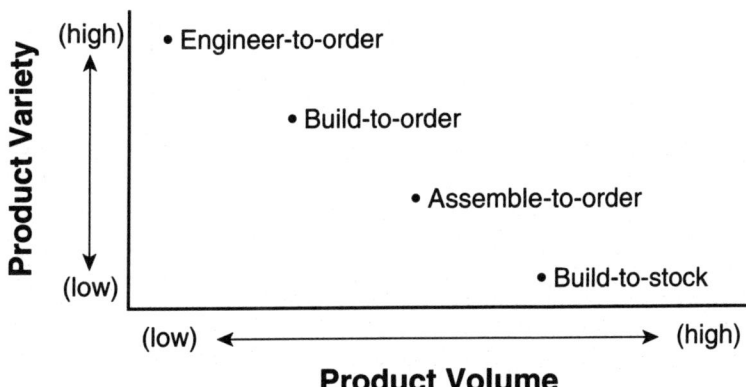

Review of Business Environments

Type of Business Environment	Description	Impact on Inventory & Forecasting
Engineer-to-order	• Requires unique one-of-a-kind engineering design • Unique bills of material and part #s • Work does not begin until customer specifications are complete • Very long lead times • One-of-a-kind products • Huge profit margin per unit	• No finished goods and little or no raw material until the customer specifications are complete • Concern—inventory costs and distribution of the product • Forecast—only revenue
Build-to-order	• More products than engineer-to-order; however, volumes are very low • Customer lead times are long, but not as long as engineer-to-order • High profit margin per unit	• Forecast revenue—no finished goods • Raw material and work-in-process inventories • Safety stock carried for long lead time items only • Concern—production schedule based on flexible facility
Assemble-to-order	• Fewer products produced than build-to-order, but volumes higher • Build to forecasted option level • Assemble option to customer specification • Use of planning bills • Medium profit margin per unit	• Little if any finished goods • Raw material held, especially for long lead time items • Concern—rapid delivery and assembly of options • Forecast—at the option level
Build-to-stock	• Very low product variety, high product volume • Build to forecasted demand of independent items • Buffer for forecast error must be calculated • Low profit margins per unit	• Inventory carried at the finished goods level • Emphasis on instant availability • Forecast—at the finished goods level

PRODUCTION AND RESOURCE PLANNING

The object of Production and Resource Planning is to link back to the manufacturing strategy and then, when approved by top management, drive the master scheduling and forecasting models.

During the business planning process, revenue is forecast. This sales forecast is based on desired market share, competitive issues, economic conditions, sales projections domestically and globally, and commercial and government orders. The sales forecasts also include forecasts for service parts and special promotions. Internal requirements for distribution, interplant orders, engineering orders, inventory build-ups, and safety stocks should be considered. The end result is the total production to meet project revenue and inventory levels for the coming year.

The basic manufacturing formula will help you visualize how business planning drives the production plan.

Step		Basic Manufacturing Formula	Units
4		Beginning Inventory	1,000
5	+	Production (Build Plan)	9,500
3	=	Available Inventory to Ship	10,500
1	−	Shipments/Sales (JIT Mastering Scheduling) (JIT Forecasting)	10,000
2	=	Ending Inventory	500

The forecasted revenue is the first step in making sure the basic manufacturing formula discussed earlier is in balance and there are adequate resources to support the production and shipment. Following are the steps in this process:

STEP 1 First, you need to establish projected shipments/sales for the year. Top executives establish the sales levels required to meet the business objectives relative to growth, market share, and so on. In this example, the projected shipment is 10,000 units.

PRODUCTION AND RESOURCE PLANNING (continued)

STEP 2 Next, you must set ending inventory levels. Inventory levels are based on two requirements:

- The desired customer level of satisfaction (that is, how many times can you ship when the customer wants the product shipped)? This topic will be discussed in detail in Module 3.

- The forecast error, which refers to the difference between forecasted sales and actual sales, and equals the fluctuation in demand (forecast error). In this example, the projected (forecasted) ending inventory level is 500 units.

STEP 3 When you have determined the desired level of shipments and projected ending inventory levels, you can determine the available to ship units by adding the shipment of 10,000 units to the projected ending inventory level of 500 units. The available inventory to ship is equal to 10,500 units.

STEP 4 The beginning inventory for the year is taken directly from the ending inventory of the previous year. In this example, it is 1,000 units.

STEP 5 You can now determine the production for the year by subtracting the beginning inventory (1,000 units) from the available to ship inventory (10,500 units). In this example, the production is 9,500 units.

NOTE: These five steps determine the accuracy of your JIT forecasting and master scheduling models.

PRODUCTION PLANNING

The **production plan** sets the overall level of manufacturing output needed to meet the planned level of sales and of inventory as documented in the business plan. The production plan acts as a control and constraint to the master production schedule (MPS). The master schedule shows when shipments are expected to occur and the required capacity for people and machines.

The purpose of the production plan is to:

- Establish the overall level of manufacturing output planned to be produced (normally stated in units, cost of sales, and sales dollar output)

- Authorize the breakdown of the production plan into specific end items and end products in the Master Schedule

- Assist the company in planning required resources

- Stabilize production and employment

A production plan allows the company to project production-by-year over the life of the business plan (for example, 1–5 years). The plan is developed during the production planning process and must be agreed upon by marketing, manufacturing, R&D, finance, and other appropriate functional groups. The plan states the planned rate of production in aggregate terms, usually by product family. It covers families or groups of products manufactured by a common manufacturing organization.

Cost of Production

The production plan is concerned not only with the number of units that need to be produced, but the cost of production as well. This cost information is required in order to determine the revenue levels needed to support this aspect of the business plan.

Base costs include carrying inventory, acquisition of materials (order or setup), stockout and backorder costs, and shrinkage (spoilage, pilferage, and obsolescence). Rate-change costs include hiring or releasing employees, additional storage facilities, and capacity-change cost. Capacity costs include overtime, part-time and temporary employees, subcontracting and outsourcing.

PRODUCTION PLANNING (continued)

The production (build) plan to meet the projected sales levels and changes in inventory levels for the coming year must have adequate resource planning to acquire the appropriate people, equipment, and material. In the long-term, acquisition of buildings and land may also be required. The process of determining the amount of resources (capacity) available is called resource planning.

Resource Planning

If there are not enough resources, adjustments must be made to fund additional acquisition, or the sales plan or inventory levels must be revised. In practice, a combination of these two alternatives is used. The process of determining if there are enough resources available is an iterative process which is driven by executives down through the organization, and then back up through the organization by the appropriate managers and other personnel.

Accurate and complete resource plans, in combination with thorough data on resource availability, allow management to set realistic production rates that are consistent with the business plan.

Resource planning involves the following steps: The production plan is broken down by major business units or groupings of products. A bill of resources is used to estimate resources, such as machine capacity, hiring of people, etc. Then bills of material (BOMs) product structure and bills of capacity are established and the required resources, labor, equipment and material are determined. The total resources are then summarized and compared to the production requirements.

Resource planning compares the demand for resources from the product groups with items included in the production plan. The resource plan indicates if there are enough resources available to meet the production plan, which in turn supports the forecasted revenue and inventory plan. This plan is prepared at least quarterly, and many times it is done on a monthly basis.

BALANCING THE IMBALANCES

If there are major imbalances between resources and planned production levels the process must be repeated until a compromise is reached which provides the resources to meet the production plan and support the revenue plan.

This iterative process of balancing the total production with the available or planned resources is critical. Once established, plans are put in place to acquire the resources and contracts are signed. These acquisitions of people, equipment, and facilities are contracted based on the assumptions that the forecasted sales will happen. This is how these resource acquisitions will be funded. Now one can begin to understand why there is such pressure to meet monthly, quarterly, and yearly shipment numbers.

When the proper level of required resources is approved, a disaggregation process takes place in which the production plan is broken down into individual reports called master production schedules.

The individual schedules then must be checked to ensure there are enough resources at the supply level to produce what has been forecasted in the master schedule.

Checking the Master Schedule

Each master schedule, with its related products and product groupings is then checked once again to ensure capacity exists to meet the individual product line revenue projections.

This checking process, also known as rough-cut capacity planning, first calculates critical resources, such as bottleneck machinery, labor shortages, and material shortages. This process produces a report called the rough-cut capacity plan, which shows any shortfalls of capacity of critical resources.

If there are no imbalances between the load of the projected sales/revenue and the available capacity, then the plan is ready for execution.

However, if shortages of critical resources do occur in one or more of the individual master schedules, the shortages must be rolled back up and adjustments made to reduce the production plan and related revenue plans and projected inventory levels, or to increase resources, such as the acquisition of more capital equipment, people, material and—most importantly—the funding required for these items.

BALANCING THE IMBALANCES (continued)

Failure to implement the checks and balances between resource planning, production planning, master scheduling, and rough-cut capacity planning will result in such things as missed shipments, low customer satisfaction, and higher inventories—and no JIT forecasting and master scheduling!

Failure to balance out the high-level production and resource plans will cause problems throughout the rest of the planning and execution process. The objectives of medium-term plans contained in the master schedules and the short-term plans contained in the material requirement plans (MRP) will not be achieved.

Once the master schedule has been checked and there is enough capacity, the MRP explosion takes place.

The material requirements plan determines a time-phased schedule of materials required to produce the units to be sold to make the revenue plan.

Resource/Capacity Strategies

An important part of the production and resource planning process is development of a capacity strategy.

When developing a manufacturing strategy to support the marketing strategy, companies must pay close attention to this capacity strategy. Decisions in this area directly impact capital expenditures.

There are three types of capacity strategies: lead, lag, and chase.

A lead capacity strategy plans for capacity well in advance of anticipated sales. Seasonal goods are an example of a lead capacity. A lag capacity, on the other hand, does not add capacity until customer demand is present. Paper products are an example of a lag capacity. The lead and lag capacity strategies are sometimes combined and referred to as a chase strategy. A tracking capacity strategy adds capacity in small amounts and attempts to closely track sales projections, thus minimizing the investment in inventory. This method is also called a level production strategy.

CONFLICTING GOALS OF STRATEGIC PLANNING

When developing the business plan and functional strategies and tradeoffs, decisions must be made by executives. In the manufacturing strategy and production plan process, things such as inventory accumulation, appropriate levels of manufacturing personnel, use of part-time and temporary personnel, plant and equipment utilization, quality, outsourcing, and new introductions need to be considered.

The sales and marketing department(s) attempt to balance high customer service, short, stable lead times, broad product line, and no missed deliveries.

The finance and accounting department(s) try to balance the objectives of minimum investment, low inventories, low capital equipment, and overhead.

And the engineering department(s) attempt to balance a focused product line and long development time.

The answer is striking the right balance in the short term as well as the long term. As a result, all of these potential conflicts must continually be addressed, evaluated, and changed if necessary. The key to making changes is the assurance that all levels in the organization have enough time to incorporate the changes in a timely, accurate and cost-effective manner.

EXERCISE 2

1. Define the following terms.

   Business Plan: _____

   _____

   Manufacturing strategy: _____

   _____

   Production plan: _____

   _____

   Resource plan: _____

   _____

2. Case study.

   In the *Inventory Management—From Warehouse to Distribution Center* book, by J. David Viale, you were hired by JADE Inc. to consult. You were so successful that the company has asked you to come back. As your first task, they have asked you to develop a business plan and the related manufacturing strategy. There is a meeting scheduled next week in which you will present the components of a business plan and formulate a manufacturing strategy.

   a) List the components of a business plan.

      _____

      _____

      _____

      _____

      _____

      _____

b) List the items that should be considered in developing a manufacturing strategy.

_____

_____

_____

_____

_____

_____

3. The Volume Variety Matrix below illustrates that when product variety increases, the product volume decreases. Fill in the appropriate type of business environments by the numbers 1–4.

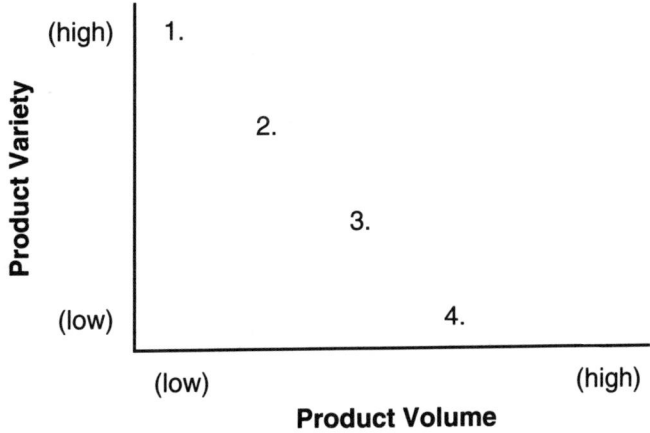

EXERCISE 2 (continued)

4. Fill in the table of Business Environments below:

Type of Business Environment	Description	Impact on Inventory & Forecasting
Engineer-to-order	• • • • • •	• • •
Build-to-order	• • • •	• • • •
Assemble-to-order	• • • • •	• • • •
Build-to-stock	• • •	• • •

5. In developing a production plan, what are the major considerations that must be made?

_____
_____
_____

6. Please complete the production planning exercise below:

   Given: Forecast   = 2000, 2500, 2000, 3000
            Beginning inventory   = 200
            Ending inventory   = 700

   Required: 1. Plan for level production and production rate
             2. Calculate inventory for each period
             3. Please write the formulas for:

Production plan =

Production rate =

Period	1	2	3	4
Beginning Inventory				
+ Production				
Available to ship				
− Forecasted sales				
= Ending Inventory				

7. List and define the three types of capacity strategies.

_____
_____
_____

EXERCISE 2 (continued)

8. What are the 10 most important things to remember about this module?

   _____

   _____

   _____

   _____

   _____

   _____

   _____

   _____

   _____

   _____

9. State the basic manufacturing formula.

   _____

   _____

   _____

   _____

   _____

10. List the steps in moving to JIT forecasting and master scheduling.

    _____

    _____

    _____

EXERCISE 2 ANSWERS

1. Definitions

   Business Plan: a statement of long-range strategy supported by projection of resources.

   Manufacturing strategy: a strategy for the manufacturing function that includes assumptions required to support the portion of the business plan devoted to long-term sales.

   Production planning: an iterative process which results in three sets of figures: Year 1 projected sales, changes in inventory levels, and production levels.

   Production plan: a plan which results in projected production-by-year over the life of the business plan.

   Resource plan: a plan which results in the determination of the amount of resources (capacity) available.

2. Case study

   a) Components of a business plan

   The following are components of a business plan. Some of these components are commonly found in business plans; some are not typically included but should be considered:

   - Mission Statement

   - Objectives

   - Customers

   - Products and Services

   - Competition

   - Current Economic and Political Environments (Environmental Scanning)

   - Distribution Channels

   - Production/Sales and Operation Plan (including the Resource Plan)

EXERCISE 2 ANSWERS (continued)

- Financial Analysis
- Major Processes
- Continuous Process Improvement (CPI) Program
- Functional Strategies
- Training and Education Strategy
- Potential Problems
- Recommendations and Implementation Plan

b) List the items that should be considered in developing a manufacturing strategy.

- Dealing with long-term market trends
- Projected growth and variability of demand
- The emergence of new technologies
- The emergence of new organization structures
- The role of information technology
- The impact of capital investment in light of shorter product life cycles
- Key competitive issues, such as time to market, time to volume, quality, costing and managing change faster and faster
- Implement the JIT Forecasting and Master Scheduling objectives to reduce the forecast error and inventory by a stated percentage and to be completed in the coming year(s).

MORE ANSWERS AHEAD

3. Fill in the Volume Variety Matrix

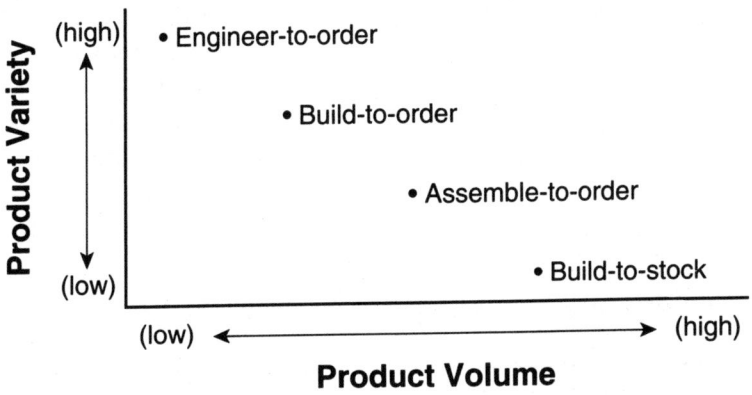

4. Major considerations in developing a production plan:

   ▶ The production plan is the end result of the executive committee's sales and inventory projections.

   ▶ Establishing total inventory levels makes it possible to manage and control the detailed levels of end items and components.

   ▶ The total of the units in the production plan must equal the sum of the individual master production schedules. The result will be the basis for master schedules that are well executed. The production plan for the coming year as well as the following years must be supported by a resource plan that details the building of facilities, selection and training of people, selection of key suppliers to ensure capacity, and a flow of materials and the acquisition of cash to fund the plan. Cash is acquired through profits, borrowing, or selling stock.

5. Fill in the Table of Business Environments below:

Type of Business Environment	Description	Impact on Inventory & Forecasting
Engineer-to-order	• Requires unique one-of-a-kind engineering design • Unique bills of material and part #s • Work does not begin until customer specifications are complete • Very long lead times • One-of-a-kind products • Huge profit margin per unit	• No finished goods and little or no raw material until the customer specifications are complete • Concern—inventory costs and distribution of the product • Forecast—only revenue
Build-to-order	• More products than engineer-to-order; however, volumes are very low • Customer lead times are long, but not as long as engineer-to-order • High profit margin per unit	• Forecast revenue—no finished goods • Raw material and work-in-process inventories • Safety stock carried for long lead time items only • Concern—production schedule based on flexible facility
Assemble-to-order	• Fewer products produced than build-to-order, but volumes higher • Build to forecasted option level • Assemble option to customer specification • Use of planning bills • Medium profit margin per unit	• Little if any finished goods • Raw material held, especially for long lead time items • Concern—rapid delivery and assembly of options • Forecast—at the option level
Build-to-stock	• Very low product variety, high product volume • Build to forecasted demand of independent items • Buffer for forecast error must be calculated • Low profit margins per unit	• Inventory carried at the finished goods level • Emphasis on instant availability • Forecast at the finished goods level

6. Production planning solution:

   Calculations:
   Production plan = Ending inventory − Beginning inventory
   + Forecasted shipments

   Production rate = Production plan/number of periods

Period	1	2	3	4
Beginning Inventory	200	700	700	1200
+ Production	2500	2500	2500	2500
Available to ship	2700	3200	3200	3700
− Forecasted sales	2000	2500	2000	3000
= Ending Inventory	700	700	1200	700

7. List and define the four types of capacity strategies.

   There are four types of capacity strategies: lead, lag, chase, and tracking.

   A lead capacity strategy plans for capacity well in advance of anticipated sales. Seasonal goods are an example of a lead capacity. A lag capacity, on the other hand, does not add capacity until customer demand is present. Paper products are an example of a lag capacity. The lead and lag capacity strategies are sometimes combined and referred to as a chase strategy. A tracking capacity strategy adds capacity in small amounts and attempts to closely track sales projections, thus minimizing the investment in inventory. This method is also called a level production strategy.

8. What are the 10 most important things to remember about this module?

   (Suggested answers)
   - Components of a business plan
   - Components of a manufacturing strategy
   - Basic manufacturing formula
   - Types of capacity strategy
   - Major considerations in developing a production planning process
   - The conflicting goals of strategic planning—checks and balances
   - Others

EXERCISE 2 ANSWERS (continued)

9. State the basic manufacturing formula.

    Beginning inventory
+ Production
= Available inventory to ship (products to sell)
− Shipments/sales
= Ending inventory

10. Steps in moving to JIT forecasting and master scheduling:

1) Develop a business plan that drives the manufacturing strategy.

2) Include objectives relating to JIT forecasting and master scheduling that include reduction of the forecast error and inventories by major products.

3) Make sure the aggregate production plan developed by the manufacturing formula process is in balance and has the high level resources, capitol equipment, facilities, people, material acquisitions properly funded. It's got to be in balance!

4) The production plan, when broken down into individual master schedules, must be in balance when they are related.

5) The capacity requirements must be adequate to meet the individual master schedules, before the individual master schedules can be re-added and matched against the total in the aggregate production plan.

MODULE III

JIT Forecasting: The Model

Learning Objectives

After completing this module, you will be able to:

- List and use five steps to develop a JIT Forecasting model

- Describe the key inventory tools that support JIT Forecasting

FORECASTED SALES

The master schedule below is a report which shows the forecasted shipments, customer orders, projected available balance (PAB), available to promise (ATP), and the Master Production Schedule. In this module the line entitled Forecasted Sales (JIT Forecasting) will be covered. The other lines in the master schedule will be covered in subsequent modules.

In this module the following topics will be covered: What is JIT Forecasting; the conflicting objectives of JIT Forecasting and how to strike a balance; why use JIT Forecasting; translating the production plan into the coming year's forecast; the steps in developing a JIT Forecasting model; and finally, other applications of the model, such as in supplier and customer environments.

Jade Ink Master Schedule						
Item: 1645ASTER Description: Pen Planning Horizon: 6 periods				Planning Fence 6 *Demand Fence 4 Lot Size — 1000		
Period	1	2	3	4	5	6
Forecasted Sales (JIT Forecasting)	360	420	340	340	240	280
Customer Orders	380	400	300	400	120	400
Projected Available Balance *(PAB) (Beginning Inventory) 800	420	20	720	320	1080	680
Available-to-Promise*	20		300		480	
Master Production Schedule* (JIT MPS)			1000		1000	
			▼		▼	

Explosion into MRP

Methods for determining these values will be covered later.

Figure 3–1: Typical Master Schedule

JIT FORECASTING OBJECTIVES

Historically, Just-in-Time principles have focused only on JIT production and JIT purchasing. However, when forecasts fluctuate (as they all do), inventories start to pile up—in finished goods, work-in-process, raw materials, and in the inventories of suppliers. The objective of this module is to develop a model for JIT Forecasting and Master Scheduling to help reduce the forecast error and the inventory levels. To prove that JIT Forecasting and Master Scheduling is not an oxymoron.

The two objectives of JIT Forecasting are:

1. To ship to customers on time, with minimum number of changes.

2. To replace a very expensive asset called "inventory" with a less-expensive asset called "information." In order to do this, the information must be timely, accurate, reliable, and consistent.

JIT Forecasting answers the question of how much inventory is needed to buffer fluctuations in forecast, customer demand, customer change orders, and supplier deliveries. If done correctly, JIT Forecasting will support the other JIT Production and Supply Chain Management Objectives. The JIT Forecasting tools and concepts presented here support contract manufacturing as well.

The major reason for any type of forecasting is to reconcile these potentially conflicting objectives:

- maximize customer service

- maximize efficiency of purchasing and production

- minimize inventory investment

- maximize profit

Reconciling these factors will bring increasing return on investment (ROI) and return on assets (ROA).

The premise of JIT Forecasting and Master Scheduling is based on the assumption that more accurate individual product-sales forecasts create smaller forecast error. Therefore, less inventory needs to be carried to maintain good customer service. Product is not built before it is needed thus avoiding the mistake of committing manufacturing resources too early. Carrying less inventory means less space is used thus saving you money.

We are talking about storing inventory with the supplier, unless there is willingness to pay expenses such as storage, insurance, and other related carrying costs. These costs are some of the major "hidden costs of manufacturing" and contribute to increasing revenues and decreasing profits (and stock prices) that many companies are facing.

THE FORECASTING MODEL

Forecasting is an interactive process that starts with the business plan (revenues, volume in dollars, capital expenditures, etc.), then is broken down into the production plan in dollar volumes and units. This total production plan is then broken down into individual master schedules in units and in dollars.

This top-down process is continually checked to ensure that enough capacity exists to meet the plan. When the process reaches the master schedule, it then starts from the bottom level and rolls back up to the business plan, to make sure the detail numbers in units and dollars still add up to the aggregate total. This process is sometimes called pyramid forecasting.

This pyramid forecasting process must also look at the time periods to be covered, the product details, and the geographical location. Following is a summary of these three types of aggregations:

- ▶ **TIME:** Long-term (months, quarters, years)—business plan; Medium-term (weeks, months)—master schedule; Short-term (days, weeks)—MRP

- ▶ **PRODUCT:** Total business volume (dollars); Families of products (dollars and units); Individual products (units); Stockkeeping units (units)

- ▶ **GEOGRAPHIC LOCATION:** Global (dollars); Regional (units/dollars); District (units); Store/Facility Volumes (units)

General Considerations in Developing a Forecasting Model

The forecasted sales included in the Master Schedule are usually stated as a monthly rate. For planning purposes, the rate must be expressed in units identical to those in the production plan described in Module 2. Master Schedules may also include the dollar amounts of the individual forecasted product sales.

The sales forecast represents sales and marketing management's best estimate of future orders. Customer orders and forecasts of future customer orders (when combined with service parts, interplant orders and warehouse needs) equal the shipment levels for the coming months, quarters, or years. This demand is referred to as independent demand (coming from outside the production factory).

Let's look at the following model and JIT Forecasting considerations.

Formula	Tools
Beginning Inventory	**Cycle Counting**
+ Build/Product (MPS)	Capacity Calculation
	Rated Capacity
	Capacity Requirements Planning (CRP)
	Material and Product Scheduling
= Available to Ship	
− Shipments − JIT Forecasting JIT Master Scheduling	Seasonality
	Averaging
	Exponential Smoothing
	Trend Analysis
	ABC Analysis
	Determine Forecast Error by Products
	Tracking Signal
= Ending Inventory	Standard Deviation of the Forecast Error
	Cycle Counting
	PAB (Projected Available Balance)
	ATP (Available to Promise)
Other Prerequisites	Accurate Documents
	Accurate Inventory

FORECAST ERROR

Every good forecast includes a projection of the forecast error. The forecast error is the difference between what you thought you were going to sell and what you actually sold. In order to improve sales forecasts, you will first need to calculate the forecast error (actual sales minus forecasted sales equals forecast error).

	1	2	3	4
Item (Product)	Actual	Forecast	Forecast Error	% Forecast Error
Pens	245	230	+15	+6.5
Pencils	110	120	−10	−8.3
Total	355	350	+5	+1.4

Figure 3-2: Year 2—Division A Products

In this example, the combined forecast error for the products (Pens and Pencils) is equal to +1.4%. Marketing people will measure success based on the total forecast error of 1.4%, whereas manufacturing people will build products based on product demand, and are therefore affected by the forecast errors of each product. The forecast error can be averaged over the history of earlier years to serve as the basis for determining what level of inventory you must carry to ensure a certain probability of shipping to a customer on time.

GOOD FORECASTS REDUCE ERROR

Improved forecasting models reduce the amount of forecast error and create fewer stockouts. Reducing error enables you to reduce inventory. Reduced forecast error also gives you your resources.

Simple forecasting models frequently provide results that are nearly as good as the more complex ones. The more elaborate mathematical models are useful only if nontechnical users can understand them and make appropriate decisions based on the results.

The advantage of simple models is that they can be understood by a greater number of people, are less expensive to implement, and can be easily applied to a wide number of manufacturing environments. Few inventory items, finished products, or management standards are important enough to justify the trouble and expense of elaborate forecasting models.

Project future demand by time period for as many periods as required by the planning system using the forecast. For example, medium-term planning spans a 12–18 month time period. The actual number of periods (months or years) will depend on your product and your industry.

Adjust individual item forecasts to coincide with forecasts of the item's group. For example, forecast options to agree with the forecast of the product on which the option is used.

Develop a model that allows for easy application of judgment factors, enabling management to correct for the effect of one-time occurrences known in advance (such as sales contests, new product announcements, market expansion, or pricing changes).

Use maintenance techniques that cut forecasting costs by reducing the need to store volumes of historical data. Three to five years of data are usually sufficient.

FIVE STEPS TO A JIT FORECASTING MODEL

When developing a JIT Forecasting model, consider including the following: 1) Establish policies and procedures and the purpose of the forecast. 2) Select the forecasting tools and techniques that find the best way to represent consistent patterns of demand, thereby improving forecast accuracy. 3) Determine how the data is going to be gathered and conditioned. 4) Test the model. 5) Establish procedures to monitor the model. Now let's look at each of these steps in more detail.

STEP 1 Establish policies and procedures. Policies and procedures should include, but not be limited to:

- What quantifiable objectives are to be met?

- What items are included in the forecast? Remember, if an item is not in the Master Production Schedule, the MRP cannot plan for it.

- When and how often is the forecast updated?

- What functional area is responsible for the forecast error/accuracy and the resultant inventory?

- Under what circumstances can the forecast be changed within the demand time fence? What level of authorization is required?

- Who pays for rush orders, premiums, and restocking charges—the customer? your company? the supplier? the entity that initiated the change?

- Do contracts describe who owns excess inventory and who pays for the related costs?

- What are other policies and procedures you would add?

If these issues are not addressed, the forecasting models and tools described in the following pages will not be as effective. Common sense must also prevail. It takes time and effort to make the changes. Quick fixes don't make it. It's been my experience that while improvement can begin immediately, real change is an evolutionary process that can take at least two years and depends upon the proper level of individual contributor and executive commitment.

STEP 2 Select the forecasting tools and techniques. These tools should represent consistent patterns of demand, thereby improving forecast accuracy.

There are many forecasting tools and techniques you can use to improve your forecasts. The tools and techniques must be part of an overall system that allows for changes in demand and is supported by policies that set guidelines to respond to these changes.

Forecasting techniques and tools are both qualitative (relying on judgment) and quantitative (relying on data). Quantitative techniques are both intrinsic and extrinsic. Intrinsic forecasting relies solely on the internal historical data of the item being forecast. Extrinsic forecasting relies on historical data of items or events related to the item being forecast. In practice, your final forecast model may be a combination of both qualitative and quantitative techniques.

QUALITATIVE TOOLS

Your judgement is valid and is one example of a qualitative forecasting technique. The following are other examples of qualitative techniques:

- **Market surveys**—Summary of preestablished data to be collected

- **Historical analogy**—For example, the sales history of black and white televisions was used to predict color TVs

- **Panel of experts**—Experts are identified in various areas and asked to forecast

- **Delphi method**—Experts are identified in various areas and asked to produce a forecast. The results of each person's forecast is shared with the entire panel, then the individual experts are asked to reformulate their forecasts.

FIVE STEPS TO A JIT FORECASTING MODEL (continued)

QUANTITATIVE TOOLS

Quantitative techniques are more fact oriented. Some examples of quantitative techniques are:

- **Moving average**—Arithmetic average

- **Exponential smoothing**—A type of weighted moving average forecasting technique

- **Market surveys**—Summary of preestablished data to be collected

- **Graphic methods**—Depictions in bar charts, pie charts, etc. of data

- **Trend projections**—Method for forecasting when an upward or downward pattern is determined

Individual forecasting tools are covered in detail later in the next module.

STEP 3 Determine how the data is to be gathered and conditioned.

Condition or filter the data—this will point out historical data problems such as missing data, extremely high or low points of demand, and the impact of large, one-time orders. Use procedures to correct the forecast of items with unusual demand patterns. This includes sporadic demand (items with periods of zero demand).

When developing a strategy for data gathering, consider the following:

1. Determine the availability and quality of the data.

2. Define the desired intrinsic patterns or the extrinsic relationships.

3. Determine the time period measured, lead times required, and customer expectations.

4. Evaluate various models for cost, accuracy, and appropriateness.

5. Establish "flags" to monitor forecast system performance.

6. Periodically reassess system performance for problems.

STEP 4 Test the model.

Before using it in practice, test the model and make adjustments as necessary.

STEP 5 Establish procedures to monitor the model.

Monitor procedures daily to ensure that the current forecast models continue to apply and that they minimize manual intervention. Expect the model to evolve over time. An effective model forecasts capacity. Incorporate the sales forecast into the model. Continue to test the forecasting model as new demand data become available. Apply an adequate level of resources—people, systems, etc.—to the process. This is the place to fix the problems.

Above all, select forecasting tools that are easy to use and understand. The most effective tools and techniques are those that are used consistently. Be sure to try out your model on historical data before implementing it.

MODULE IV

JIT Forecasting: The Tools

Learning Objectives

After completing this module, you will be able to:

- Describe the key forecasting tools

- Describe the key inventory tools

- Use each of the tools to calculate answers to several problems

FORECASTING TOOLS

There are many tools and techniques that can be used to improve forecasting. Because more complex tools do not produce significantly better results, you will be learning about the following quantitative tools: Seasonality, straight averaging, moving average, weighted moving average, and exponential smoothing.

Calculating Seasonality

Once you have annual sales figures, factor in seasonal changes in sales, such as changes by quarter or holiday periods: For example, historically, in the semiconductor industry, third quarter figures typically increase.

The purpose of using the seasonality forecasting tool is to reflect the fact that annual sales take place on a seasonal basis.

To calculate the seasonality index for each quarter or month:

1. Obtain sales history numbers from your history files for a given year.

2. Divide the total of sales history numbers by the number of quarters (4) or months (12).

3. Divide the sales history number for each quarter by the average quarterly sales. The resulting figure equals your seasonality index.

In the exercise that follows, you will calculate seasonality based on quarterly data.

EXERCISE 3

DIRECTIONS:

1. In this exercise you will be calculating seasonality by quarter for Company XYZ. We have given you the sales history figures. Use the accompanying instructions to assist you with your calculations.

2. After you have completed the calculations, identify the business questions you would ask.

Column	What to do
#1	Enter sales history figures for Year 1 from the history files. We have entered these.
#2	To calculate the Average Quarterly Sales, divide the total from column 1 (250) by 4 (which represents 4 quarters), and enter this figure in column 2. We have done this.
#3	To calculate the Seasonality Index for each quarter, divide each quarterly figure in column 1 by each quarterly figure in column 2, and enter the answers in column 3. We have done the first quarter for you.
#4	Sales history figures for Year 2 are provided in column 4.

Seasonality Worksheet
Company XYZ

	1	2	3	4	5	6	7	8	9
	Year 1 (19XX)			Year 2 (19XX)			Year 3 (19XX)		
Qtr	Sales History	Avg. Qtrly Sales	Seasonality Index (as a %)	Sales History	Avg. Qtrly Sales	Seasonality Index (as a %)	Projected Avg. Seasonality for Year 3	Avg. Qtrly Sales	Projected Sales for Year 3
1	50	62.5	.80	75					
2	100	62.5		125					
3	25	62.5		50					
4	75	62.5		100					
Total	250			350					450

5. To calculate Average Quarterly Sales for Year 2, follow instructions similar to those provided for column 2.

6. To calculate Seasonality Index for Year 2, follow instructions provided for column 3.

7. For each quarter, calculate the Projected Average Seasonality for Year 3 by adding column 3 plus column 6, then dividing this total by 2. This gives you an average of past seasonality.

8. To calculate the Average Quarterly Sales for Year 3, divide the Projected Sales Total for Year 3 (450) by 4 (4 quarters), and enter the answer in column 8.

9. To calculate the Seasonally Adjusted Projected Quarterly Sales, multiply column 7 by column 8, and enter the answer in column 9.

EXERCISE 3 ANSWERS

Seasonality Worksheet
Company XYZ

	1	2	3	4	5	6	7	8	9
	Year 1 (19XX)			Year 2 (19XX)			Year 3 (19XX)		
Qtr	Sales History	Avg. Qtrly Sales	Seasonality Index (as a %)	Sales History	Avg. Qtrly Sales	Seasonality Index (as a %)	Projected Avg. Seasonality for Year 3	Avg. Qtrly Sales	Projected Sales for Year 3
1	50	62.5	.80	75	87.5	.86	.83	112.5	93.38
2	100	62.5	1.6	125	87.5	1.43	1.52	112.5	171.00
3	25	62.5	.40	50	87.5	.57	.48	112.5	54.00
4	75	62.5	1.2	100	87.5	1.14	1.17	112.5	131.63
Total	250			350					450

2. Suggested business questions:

   - What type of adjustments to manufacturing (specifically to capacity) do you need to make?

   - What type of quarterly fluctuations do you have in your forecast error?

   - How does seasonality impact your suppliers?

USING INTRINSIC FORECASTING TOOLS

You will use the following intrinsic forecasting tools in this book: Straight averaging, Moving average, Weighted moving average, Exponential smoothing

Straight Averaging

This is a mathematical average of a specific number of periods. To get a straight average, each new period is added to the total of the prior periods and then divided by the number of periods included.

Example: 3- and 4-Period Straight Averages

$$\text{Formula: } \frac{\Sigma \text{ (Sum of) D (Demand)}}{\text{N (number of periods*)}}$$

$$\frac{\overset{\text{Period 1}}{100} + \overset{\text{Period 2}}{90} + \overset{\text{Period 3}}{110}}{3} = \frac{300}{3} = 100$$

$$\frac{\overset{\text{Period 1}}{100} + \overset{\text{Period 2}}{90} + \overset{\text{Period 3}}{110} + \overset{\text{Period 4}}{180}}{4} = \frac{480}{4} = 120$$

* Such as months, year

Advantage: Very easy to understand

Disadvantage: Responsiveness decreases with time

USING INTRINSIC FORECASTING TOOLS (continued)

Moving Average

This is a mathematical average of a specific number of the most recent periods. As each new period is added, the oldest one is dropped. For example, it's common to have 3 or 5 periods included in the moving average. The number of periods will be impacted by the length of the product life cycle.

Example: 3-Period Moving Average

$$\text{Formula: } \frac{\Sigma D}{N}$$

$$\frac{\overset{\text{Period 1}}{100} + \overset{\text{Period 2}}{90} + \overset{\text{Period 3}}{110}}{3} = \frac{300}{3} = 100$$

$$\frac{\overset{\text{Period 2}}{90} + \overset{\text{Period 3}}{110} + \overset{\text{Period 4}}{180}}{3} = \frac{380}{3} = 127$$

Advantage: More responsive

Disadvantage: All demands have equal value until dropped

Weighted Average

This is an averaging technique in which the data to be averaged are weighted. Typically, the weights are greatest for the most current periods. The weights must always add up to 1.00 or 100 percent. See weighted moving average example on the next page for further explanation.

Weighted Moving Average

The following examples illustrate a combination of moving and weighted averaging techniques. How do you establish the weighting factor? By using a combination of judgement, guessing, testing or using historical data.

Example: 3-Period Weighted Moving Average

Weights:

	Period 1	Period 2	Period 3	
	100 +	90 +	110	=
	*20% +	30% +	50%	= 100%
	.2 × 100 = 20	.3 × 90 = 27	.5 × 110 = 55	= 102

Note: *The percentages 20%, 30%, 50% are based on judgement (management, yours, etc.) The development of appropriate weights can be done by analyzing prior data or with an educated intuition.

Example: Updated 3-Period Weighted Moving Average

Period 1	Period 2	Period 3	Period 4	
100 +	90 +	110 +	180	
	.2 × 90 = 18	.3 × 110 = 33	.5 × 180 = 90	= 141

Advantage: Newest data counts most; shows a trend

Disadvantage: A little more complex

EXERCISE 4

DIRECTIONS:

In this exercise you will be calculating three types of averages—

1. Calculate the straight average for 6 periods.

2. Calculate the moving average for 3 periods.

3. Calculate the weighted moving average for 3 periods.

Weighting Assumptions:

- Year-1 = .5

- Year-2 = .3

- Year-3 = .2

Straight, Moving, and Weighted Moving Average Worksheet
Division A of Company XYZ
Product A: Year 3 Forecast

	1	2	3	4	5	6
Period	Historical Actual Sales	Forecasted Sales	Forecast Error	Straight Average	Moving Avg. 3 Period	Weighted Moving Avg. 3 Period
−6	153	151	+2			
−5	149	150	−1			
−4	151	150	+1			
−3	152	150	+2			
−2	147	151	−4			
−1	151	150	+1			
0		150				
Total						

Why are your answers so close to each other?

EXERCISE 4 ANSWERS

Straight, Moving, and Weighted Moving Average Worksheet
Division A of Company XYZ
Product A: Year 3 Forecast

Period	1 Historical Actual Sales	2 Forecasted Sales	3 Forecast Error	4 Straight Average	5 Moving Avg. 3 Period	6 Weighted Moving Avg. 3 Period
−6	153	151	+2			
−5	149	150	−1			
−4	151	150	+1			
−3	152	150	+2			
−2	147	151	−4			
−1	151	150	+1			
0		150		150.5	150	150
Total	903					

How to Get the Answers

▶ **For straight averaging:**

- Add the figures in column 1 and enter the Total.

- Divide the column 1 Total by the total number of periods (6).

- Enter your answer in column 4.

▶ **For a 3 period moving average:**

- Add periods -1, -2, -3 and divide this total by 3.

- Enter your answer in column 5.

EXERCISE 4 ANSWERS

▶ **For a 3 period weighted moving average:**

- Multiply each given weighting factor by the historical actual sales data for each corresponding year.

    Year -1: .5 × 151 = 75.5
    Year -2: .3 × 147 = 44.1
    Year -3: .2 × 152 = 30.4
                                           150.0

- Enter your answer in column 6.

Why are your answers so close to each other?

Answer: Because the forecast error is so small.

CALCULATING EXPONENTIAL SMOOTHING

Exponential Smoothing

This is another type of averaging technique in which past periods are weighted. The heaviest weight is assigned to the most recent data. The smoothing is termed "exponential" because data points are weighted according to an exponential function of their age.

The alpha factor (α) is a weighting factor, also known as a smoothing constant. The value of the alpha factor is between 0 and 1.00. The alpha factor is determined by trial and error as you apply different alpha factors to the most recent data.

Full stability (when there is no variation in sales from year to year). What food products do you think would have full stability? In the U.S., an example would be bread consumption. In Ireland, an example would be potato consumption. In the Far East, an example would be rice.

Full response (when there is a wide variation in sales from year to year): What food product in the U.S. would have full response? An example of full response for a nonfood product would be certain software packages.

EXAMPLES: **Calculating Full Stability and Full Response**

Remember, whenever parentheses are bracketed, you do the calculation within the parentheses first.

New Forecast = Old Forecast + [α × (actual demand − old forecast)]
New Forecast = 100 + [α × (180 − 100)]

For full stability: $\alpha = 0$

(Coming year = 100 − 0 × 80 = 100)
New Forecast = 100 + [0 × (180 − 100)]
New Forecast = 100

For full response: $\alpha = 1.0$

New Forecast = 100 + [1.0 × (180 − 100)] 100 + 1 (80)
 100 + 80 = 180
New Forecast = 180 equal to new value

CALCULATING EXPONENTIAL SMOOTHING (continued)

Note: The determination of the alpha factor is a trial and error process in which you ask yourself the question: Is your forecast error too large? If so, increase the alpha factor. If not, use the existing alpha factor to establish inventory level.

The following figure is an example of forecasting sales for 1997 using the exponential smoothing technique. Would you say that the forecast error is too large?

Assume that the 1993 old forecast plus the actual demand are the same given 21.

Alpha Factor (α) = 0.1

	Given	**Exponential Smoothing Formula**						
Year	Actual Sales (millions)	Old Forecast	+	[α × (Actual Demand − Old Forecast)] Sales (millions)				= New Forecast
1994	26	21	+	(21	−	21) =	0	
		21	+ .1 ×	0				= 21
1995	33	21	+	(26	−	21) =	5	
		21	+ .1 ×	5				= 21.5
1996	34	21.5	+	(33	−	21.5) =	11.5	
		21.5	+ .1 ×	11.5				= 22.7
1997	50	22.7	+	(34	−	22.7) =	11.3	
		22.7	+ .1 ×	11.3				= 23.8

Figure 4-1: 1997 Sales Forecast Using Exponential Smoothing

Is the alpha factor too large or too small? Discuss possible solutions.

USING EXTRINSIC FORECASTING TOOLS

Extrinsic indicators are supplied by such bodies as government agencies and trade associations. The data must be assigned a period number in order to associate it with group demand data for the same period. Some examples of indicators are gross national product, industry sales, inventories, housing starts, retail sales, price index, and unemployment rate.

Extrinsic forecasting assumes that the relationship between demand and some external factor (e.g., housing starts) will hold into the future, and that a forecast of the external factor can therefore be used as a basis for a demand forecast.

External indicators can also come from internal sources. The size of the sales backlog of one product group may indicate later sales of some associated product line—for example, sales of automobiles will occur some months in advance of sales of spare parts. The shipments of the automobiles would then be called a "leading indicator" for the sales of the spare items.

This type of forecasting is more appropriate for larger groups (product lines) than for individual products (e.g., all adults' clothes, all investment castings, all small motors).

Extrinsic forecasting is usually applied to individual major products. The higher expense of developing extrinsic forecasting models normally limits its use to a few groups.

Types of Extrinsic Forecasting

- *Regression analysis*—Describes the relationship between one item and one or more independent variables. In regression analysis a relationship is established whereby the value of one variable can be predicted given the knowledge of other variables. This tool is useful in aggregate forecasting. Aggregate forecasting is a total forecast for all products. Disaggregate forecasting is done for single products. The simplest version of regression analysis is "trend line analysis."

- *Double exponential smoothing*—A method of exponential smoothing for trend situations. This method, also called second-order smoothing, uses two previously computed averages to extrapolate into the future.

- *Triple smoothing*—A method of exponential smoothing for an accelerating or decelerating trend such as in a fad cycle.

- *Trend analysis*—A method of forecasting sales when upward and downward trends exist.

FORECASTING METHODS

Now that we've learned some forecasting methods, how do we know when to use them? We refer to the product life cycle first discussed in Module I. The life cycle is depicted below followed by a list of forecasting methods used at each point in the life cycle.

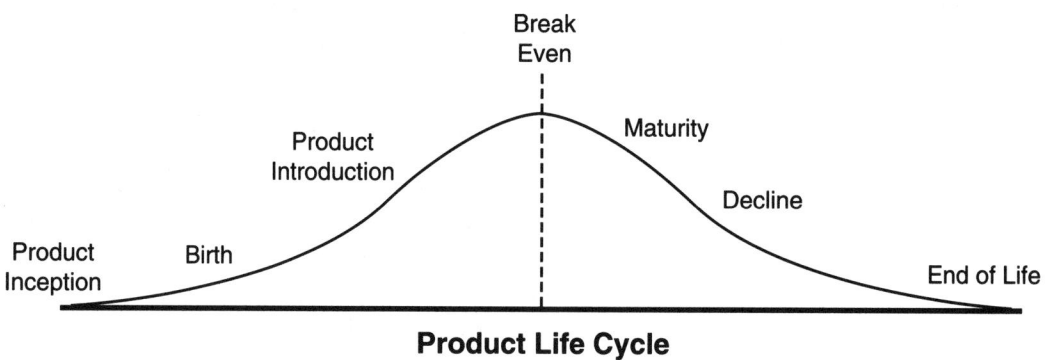

Product Life Cycle

▶ **New Product Introduction**

    Weighted moving average
    Delphi method
    Historical analogy
    Trend projection—regression analysis
    Judgement

▶ **Growth and Maturity**

    Exponential smoothing
    Multiple regression
    Market surveys

▶ **Decline**

    Judgemental/Opinions
    Market Surveys
    Historical analogy

▶ **End of Life (EOL)**

    Historical analogy

THE KEY TO JIT FORECASTING

Since all forecasts have a forecast error, the next question is how to set the finished goods inventory level. This is done by calculating the amount of inventory needed to buffer this forecast error and meet the company's objective of on time shipment (i.e., customer service level).

One of the most important tools used in determining the required inventory is the "Standard Deviation of the Forecast Error" calculation. The purpose of this calculation is to: *Calculate an amount of inventory that will allow for the forecast error and establish a certain probability of still shipping on time.*

This inventory is called safety stock, and is a quantity of stock to keep in inventory to protect against unexpected fluctuations in demand or supply. It is usually carried at the finished goods level. However, sometimes it is used to compensate for scrap and obsolete parts. Hard-to-get parts are carried as safety stock to guard against unreliable supplier deliveries. Safety lead time —which simply is an inflation of the lead time—is used sometimes to buffer against customer changes in the original lead time. Safety lead time and safety stock have the same effect on inventory; they both create demand for inventory before it is needed.

CALCULATING THE STANDARD DEVIATION OF FORECAST ERROR

The following is an example of how to calculate the standard deviation of the forecast error.

The table below shows how to calculate the forecast error and the standard deviation of the forecast error.

History of Product A

Time periods*	1 Actual Sales	2 Forecast	3 Forecast error	4 Forecast error^2 (squared)
1	1520	1510	+10	100
2	1490	1500	−10	100
3	1510	1500	+10	100
4	1520	1500	+20	400
5	1470	1510	−40	1600
6	1510	1500	+10	100
			Total	2400

*Time period could be months or years

Steps for Calculating the Standard Deviation of the Forecast Error

STEP 1 To calculate forecast error, subtract column 2 from column 1 and enter the results in column 3.

STEP 2 Square each period's forecast error (column 3 × column 3) and enter the results in column 4. Remember, when you square a number you multiply the number by itself.

STEP 3 Add all the entries in column 4. The total equals 2400.

STEP 4 Calculate the average of the square of the deviation by dividing the square of the deviation by the number of time periods. (2400 ÷ 6 = 400).

STEP 5 Now find the square root sign ($\sqrt{}$) on your calculator, and determine the square root of 400. The answer is 20.

The steps noted above translate into the following formula for Standard Deviation:

Σ = sum of
A = actual results
F = forecast
N = # of periods used in the forecast
i = each time period

$$\text{Standard deviation} = \sqrt{\frac{\Sigma (A_i - F_i)^2}{N - 1}}$$

or

$$= \sqrt{\frac{\Sigma (A_i - F_i)^2}{N}}$$

Note: N or N − 1. Use N with a large population (> 30)
Use N − 1 with a sample or a small (≤ 30) population

CALCULATING THE STANDARD DEVIATION OF FORECAST ERROR (continued)

The Answer

The answer you should get is 20, which is the square root of 400. The answer, 20, is stated as one positive standard deviation. What this means is that if 20 units of inventory (safety stock) were held to buffer against the forecast error, a certain level of on-time shipments would have a high probability of happening. Notice how small the inventory level is; this is because of the small forecast error.

The 20 units equal one positive standard deviation, and if this amount were to be carried in inventory, the probability of on-time shipments would be 84 out of 100 times, or 84% of the time. The 84% (.843) comes from the Customer Service level table shown in Figure 4-2, below.

For most customers, this would be totally unacceptable, and the supplier would be forced to carry at least two or three positive standard deviations, which would result in doubling or tripling the inventory investment—from 20 units to 40 units to 60 units. The result would be to increase the number of on-time shipments from 84% to 97.5% to 99.85% of the time (refer to Figure 4-2 below).

Notice that as the inventory doubles and then triples, the on-time shipments increase at a diminishing rate.

Inventory level (units)	Standard deviation	Mean absolute deviation	Customer service level*
0	0.00	0.00	.50
20	1.00	1.25	.843
40	2.00	2.50	.975
60	3.00	3.75	.9985

This data is a statistical given.

Figure 4-2: Modified Customer Service Level Table

CALCULATING THE MEAN ABSOLUTE DEVIATION (MAD)

MAD is a shortcut method for calculating the standard deviation of the forecast error, which will provide approximately the same answer as the standard deviation of the forecast error.

To calculate MAD, simply total the forecast error, disregarding whether the forecast error is negative or positive. This total is then divided by the number of time periods being reviewed. The following calculation of MAD is shown in Figure 3-3 on page 74.

Bias is a term for the pattern of forecast errors (deviation) from the mean, either consistently too high or consistently too low. A good forecasting model should contain little or no bias.

History of Product A

	1	2	3	4
Time periods*	Actual sales	Forecast	Forecast error	Forecast error^2 (squared)
1	1520	1510	+10	100
2	1490	1500	−10	100
3	1510	1500	+10	100
4	1520	1500	+20	400
5	1470	1510	−40	1600
6	1510	1500	+10	100
		Total	100	2400

*Time period could be months or years

CALCULATING THE MEAN ABSOLUTE DEVIATION (MAD) (continued)

Steps for Calculating Mean Absolute Deviation (MAD)

STEP 1 Using the table, add the forecast error in column 3, disregarding the negative and positive signs (10 + 10 + 20 + 40 + 10 = 100).

STEP 2 Calculate the average of 100 by dividing 100 by the number of time periods (100 ÷ 6 = 16.7 rounded to 16).

STEP 3 Multiply 16 × 1.25 (the MAD factor for one positive deviation) = 20, which is equal to one standard deviation.

Note: The relationship between MAD and the standard deviation is MAD × 1.25, 250, 3.75, etc.

Inventory level (units)	Standard deviation	Mean absolute deviation	Customer service level
0	0.00	0.00	.50
20	1.00	1.25	.843
40	2.00	2.50	.975
60	3.00	3.75	.9985

Figure 4-2: Modified Customer Service Level Table

To ship to customers 100% of the time (99.99967), the inventory would have to be increased six-fold (six positive deviations, aka 6 sigma) from 20 units to 120 units. Since going from three standard deviations to six will only increase your shipment levels by less than 1% but require doubling of the inventory from 60 to 120, companies may opt not to ship 100% of the time.

Remember, these inventory levels (20, 40, 60, 80 increments of 20 in this example) represent one positive deviation. If you don't like the answer, try improving your forecast model—and reducing your forecast error—by using the forecast model discussed in this module.

USING A TRACKING SIGNAL TO TEST YOUR FORECASTING MODEL

So far, you have a forecast model that includes seasonality, weighted moving average, exponential smoothing, and standard deviation of the forecast error. Now we will introduce you to another tool.

The tracking signal is used to measure the "health" of your forecasting model. This measure is calculated by dividing the sum of the period forecast error by the mean absolute deviation. Tracking signal is computed as the ratio of the cumulative error to the MAD. If the answer is greater than +4.0 or –4.0, you need to review the forecast model.

THE 80/20 RULE (ABC ANALYSIS)

This law was discovered by Pareto, an Italian economist. He discovered that a small percentage of a population always has the greatest effect on the entire population. Pareto's law was further expanded to the ABC classification, and is summarized below. When considering how to apply this tool to establish inventory levels, consider the following: "Which products (and which customers) generate 80 percent of the revenue?" Answer: Approximately 20 percent of the products and customers generate 80 percent of the revenue.

ABC Analysis

Percent of customers, products, or parts	Generates what percentage of the company's revenue and inventory investment?	These are called
20%	80%	"A" customers "A" products "A" parts
30%	15%	"B" customers "B" products "B" parts
50%	5%	"C" customers "C" products "C" parts

Note that the A customers still want the same level of shipments of your B and C products as they receive from the A products.

The fluctuation in demand for the B and C products causes many of the product mix problems, changes on the shop floor (capacity), and changes in supplier due dates. Some companies build C products during the slower times of the quarter. This causes an inventory build-up, but it is felt that this is more than offset by the flexibility gained in capacity at the end of the quarter.

To put the ABC analysis to practical use, consider doing the following:

- ❑ Reduce the forecast error by improving the forecast model.
- ❑ For A customers and A and B parts, use the standard deviation formula.
- ❑ For C parts, give a predetermined number of days' supply and allow the production floor to build this during slower periods of each quarter.

The standard deviation of forecast error tool can also be used to determine

- ✔ The amount of extra (safety) lead time needed to ensure on-time delivery to customers or from suppliers.

- ✔ The amount of work to release to the shop floor to make sure machines do not run out of work. That is, how much "queue" (buffer) is needed in back of the bottleneck work center. This technique would primarily be used in a build-to-order or assemble-to-order environment.

- ✔ The number of extra (buffer) pieces to start to ensure a particular yield (for example, scrap allowance).

- ✔ The amount of machine downtime (safety) to allow for planning utilization of available capacity.

EXERCISE 5

You are now going to go through a process of developing a forecasting model for JADE Inc. Below are things they asked you to do.

1. In your own words describe the three components of JIT, as described in this module.

2. Describe the two major objectives of JIT Forecasting.

3. Describe the five steps in developing a forecasting model.

4. List five qualitative forecasting techniques.

5. List four quantitative forecasting techniques.

_____

_____

_____

_____

6. When you condition or filter data, you are looking for what are called outliers. Types of Outlier are data errors, unusual demand, loss of data, permanent changes in demand.

Outlier Exercise:

Product	Month					
	July	August	September	October	November	December
Pen (Fine)	500	1640	820	8200	1620	
Pen (Med.)	540	1660	860	540	1600	
Pencil (Hard)	320	1280	540	320	1200	
Pencil (Med.)	460	1840	660	?	1600	
Pencil (Soft)	580	600	580	590	600	
Total						

From the data above, answer the following:

Assume that seasonality for July, August and September will repeat itself in October, November and December, with the exception of Pencil (soft), which has instant sales.

a. What is forecast for December? _____

For each product? _____

For total? _____

b. What actions should be taken? (Include corrections to the table above)

_____

_____

EXERCISE 5 (continued)

7. List the steps in calculating seasonality and then calculate the seasonality for the pen and pencil products.

   _____

   _____

   _____

8. Write the formula for exponential smoothing.

   _____

   _____

   _____

9. Describe the role of safety stock.

   _____

   _____

   _____

   _____

   _____

10. Calculate the average seasonality for Product Pen and Product Pencil.

    Product Pen: Next year's sales = 150

    Product Pencil: Next year's sales = 300

    Note: For the sake of simplicity, the same seasonality factors will be used for both Products Pen and Pencil. In practice, individual seasonality indexes can be determined for each product.

Product Pen

Quarter	Avg. Qtrly Sales	Avg. Seasonality Index	Projected Sales for Year 3
1		.83	
2		1.52	
3		.48	
4		1.17	
	150		150

Product Pencil

Quarter	Avg. Qtrly Sales	Avg. Seasonality Index	Projected Sales for Year 3
1		.83	
2		1.52	
3		.48	
4		1.17	
	300		300

From this exercise, what have you learned about seasonality?

_____

_____

_____

11. List the steps for calculating standard deviation of the forecast error.

_____

_____

_____

EXERCISE 5 (continued)

12. List the steps for calculating mean absolute deviation.

_____

_____

_____

_____

13. In your conversation with the management team of JADE Inc. they have indicated a desired customer service level of shipping to customers 100% of the time. They then handed you the table on the next page listing their historical sales and forecast data for the last ten periods.

The following is required:

a. Write the formula for standard deviation.

_____

_____

b. Calculate one positive standard deviation from the table below.

_____

_____

c. Then determine the amount of inventory JADE would need to carry to obtain the level of customer satisfaction desired by the JADE management team.

_____

_____

d. List alternatives to the answer in 13(c) above.

_____

_____

e. Fill in the table below.

Time Period	Forecast	Sales	Forecast Error	Forecast Error²
1	500	600		
2	500	500		
3	500	400		
4	500	450		
5	500	700		
6	500	600		
7	500	550		
8	500	500		
9	500	350		
10	500	450		
Total	5,000	5,100		

14. Calculate exponential smoothing using an alpha factor of $\alpha = 0.3$. Assume that the 1989 old forecast plus the actual demand equals 21.

Exponential Smoothing Formula

Year	Actual Sales (millions)	Old Forecast	+	[α × (Actual Demand − Old Forecast)] Sales (millions)	= New Forecast
1990	26	21	+	.3 ×	
			+	.3 ×	
1991	33		+		
			+	.3 ×	
1992	34		+		
			+	.3 ×	
1993	50		+		
			+	.3 ×	

Is the forecast error too large or too small?

Is the alpha factor too large or too small?

EXERCISE 5 (continued)

15. List the steps in moving to a JIT forecasting model. Include those from Module II.

_____

_____

_____

_____

_____

_____

_____

_____

_____

EXERCISE 5 ANSWERS

1. In your own words describe the three components of JIT, as described in this module.
   - JIT Production
   - JIT Purchasing
   - JIT Forecasting

2. Describe the two major objectives of JIT Forecasting.

   ❑ To ship to customer on time, with minimum numbers of changes.

   ❑ To replace a very expensive asset called "inventory" with a less-expensive asset called "information."

3. Describe the five steps in developing a forecasting model.

   1) Establish policies and procedures and the purpose of the forecast;

   2) Select the forecasting tools and techniques that find the best way to represent consistent patterns of demand, thereby improving forecast accuracy;

   3) Determine how the data is going to be gathered and conditioned;

   4) Test the module;

   5) Establish procedures to monitor the model.

4. List five qualitative forecasting techniques.
   - Market survey
   - Historical analogy
   - Panel of experts
   - Delphi method
   - Expert opinion

EXERCISE 5 ANSWERS (continued)

5. List four quantitative forecasting techniques.
   - Moving average
   - Graphic method
   - Trend projections
   - Exponential smoothing

6. When you condition or filter data, you are looking for what is called outliers. Following are types of outliers (data errors, unusual demand, loss of data, permanent changes in demand):

Outlier Exercise:

Product	Month					
	July	August	September	October	November	December
Pen (Fine)	500	1600	820	500	1620	820
Pen (Med.)	540	1660	860	540	1600	860
Pencil (Hard)	320	1280	540	320	1200	540
Pencil (Med.)	460	1840	660	460	1600	660
Pencil (Soft)	580	600	580	590	600	590
Total						3,470

1. What is forecast for December? For each product? For total?

2. What actions should be taken? (Open discussion).

Pen (fine): October figure of 8200 is incorrect—replace with the figure of 500, which represents the same figure as the first month of last quarter.

Pen (medium), pencil (hard lead), and pencil (medium lead) projections for December would all be based on the seasonal figures for the last quarter.

Pencil (soft)—which does not display any seasonality, would have a December forecast based on the average of the prior five months.

7. List the steps in calculating seasonality and then calculate the seasonality for the pen and pencil products.

   To calculate the seasonality index for each quarter or month:

   a. Obtain sales history numbers from your history files for a given year.

   b. Divide the total of sales history numbers by the number of quarters (4) or months (12).

   c. Divide the sales history number for each quarter by the average quarterly sales. The resulting figure equals your seasonality index.

   Show answers here.

8. Write the formula for exponential smoothing.

   Remember, when you have parentheses which are bracketed, you do the calculation within the parentheses first.

   New forecast = Old forecast + [α × (actual demand − old forecast)]

9. Describe the role of safety stock.

   Safety stock is a quantity of stock to keep in inventory to protect against unexpected fluctuations in demand or supply. It is usually carried at the finished goods level. However, sometimes it is used to compensate for scrap and obsolete parts. Hard-to-get parts are carried as safety stock to guard against unreliable supplier deliveries. Safety lead time—which simply is an inflation of the lead time—is sometimes used to buffer against customer changes in the original lead time. Safety lead time and safety stock have the same effect on inventory; they both create demand for inventory before it is needed.

EXERCISE 5 ANSWERS (continued)

10. Product Pen

Quarter	Avg. Qtrly Sales	Avg. Seasonality Index	Projected Sales for Year 3
1	37.5	.83	31
2	37.5	1.52	57
3	37.5	.48	18
4	37.5	1.17	44
	150		150

Product Pencil

Quarter	Avg. Qtrly Sales	Avg. Seasonality Index	Projected Sales for Year 3
1	75	.83	62
2	75	1.52	114
3	75	.48	36
4	75	1.17	88
	300		300

From this exercise, what have you learned about seasonality?

Suggested answer: The exercise showed

- How you will ship product by quarter or month.

- How to project production and changes in inventory levels from quarter to quarter or month to month.

11. Steps for Calculating Standard Deviation of the Forecast Error

1) To calculate forecast error, subtract actual results from forecast.

2) Square each period's forecast error. Remember, when you square a number, you multiply the number by itself.

3) Add the answers from step 2.

4) Calculate the average of the square of the deviation by dividing the square by the number of time periods.

5) Now find the square root sign ($\sqrt{}$) on your calculator, and determine the square root of your answer in step 4.

12. List the steps for calculating mean absolute deviation.

    Mean Absolute Deviation (MAD) is the average (mean) of the differences (deviations) between the forecast and the actual sales, taking no account of plus or minus signs (using absolute values).

    Note: The relationship between the MAD and the standard deviation is approximately: 1 positive Sigma = 1.25 × MAD.

13. Your completed table should look like the one below:

    a. Standard Deviation: $\dfrac{100,000}{10} = 10,000$

    $\sqrt{10,000} = 100$

    b. MAD = $\dfrac{800}{10} = 80 \times 1.25 = 100$

    e. Fill in the table below.

Time Period	Forecast	Sales	Forecast Error	Forecast Error^2
1	500	600	100	10,000
2	500	500	0	0
3	500	400	−100	10,000
4	500	450	−50	2,500
5	500	700	200	40,000
6	500	600	100	10,000
7	500	550	50	2,500
8	500	500	0	0
9	500	350	−150	22,500
10	500	450	50	2,500
Total	5,000	5,100		100,000

EXERCISE 5 ANSWERS (continued)

14. $\alpha = 0.3$

Exponential Smoothing Formula

Year	Actual Sales (millions)	Old Forecast	+	[α × (Actual Demand − Old Forecast)] Sales (millions)			= New Forecast
1990	26	21	+	.3 × (21 −	21) =	0	
		21	+	.3 ×	0		= 21
1991	33	21	+	(26 −	21) =	5	
		21	+	.3 ×	5		= 22.5
1992	34	22.5	+	(33 −	22.5) =	10.5	
		22.5	+	.3 ×	10.5		= 25.7
1993	50	25.7	+	(34 −	25.7) =	8.3	
		25.7	+	.3 ×	8.3		= 28.2

The forecast error is too large. The alpha factor is still too small.

15. Steps to moving to a JIT Forecasting model:

1) Develop a business plan that drives the manufacturing strategy.

2) Include objectives relating to JIT Forecasting and Master Scheduling that include reduction of the forecast error and inventories by major products.

3) Make sure the aggregate production plan developed by the manufacturing formula process is in balance and has the high level resources, capital equipment, facilities, people, material acquisitions properly funded. It's got to be in balance!

4) The production plan, when broken down into individual master schedules, must be in balance when they are re-added.

5) The capacity requirements must be adequate to meet the individual master schedules, before the individual master schedules can be re-added and matched against the total in the aggregated Production Plan.

6) Establish policies and procedures and the purpose of the forecast. What quantifiable objectives are to be met?

7) Select the forecasting tools and techniques that find the best way to represent consistent patterns of demand, thereby improving forecast accuracy.

8) Determine how the data is going to be gathered and conditioned.

9) Test the module.

10) Establish procedures to monitor the model to ensure that the current forecast model continues to apply.

MODULE V

JIT Master Scheduling

Learning Objectives

After completing this module, you will be able to:

- List the six steps in developing a Master Schedule

- Calculate Available-to-Promise and Projected Available Balance

- Define the four major manufacturing environments and explain how the master schedule applies to each

WHY JIT MASTER SCHEDULING?

Master scheduling and demand management involve: receiving customer orders, determining forecasted shipment levels, setting the finished goods inventory level, developing Master Schedule and testing the Master Schedule through rough-cut capacity planning.

The forecasting portion of the master schedule can provide stability to material planning by increasing the forecast accuracy and reducing the schedule "nervousness." As a result, costly expediting can be minimized.

In addition to forecasts and customer orders, this schedule contains the available-to-promise and projected available inventory balances. The output of the master schedule is the line called the Master Production Schedule (MPS). The amounts on this line are used to drive the material requirements plan (MRP).

Finally, the master schedule can ensure execution of the production plan by developing the production schedule, managing and controlling production processes, structuring and controlling time fences and lead times, and adjusting for other seasonal requirements.

Figure 5-1 below is an example of a master schedule.

Jade Inc.
Master Schedule

Item: 1645ASTER
Description: Pen
Planning Horizon: 6 periods

Planning Fence: 6 periods
Demand Fence: 3 periods
Lot Size — 1000

Period	1	2	3	4	5	6
Forecasted Sales (JIT Forecasting)	360	420	340	340	240	280
Customer Orders	380	400	300	400	120	400
Projected Available Balance* (Beginning Inventory) 800	420	20	720	320	1080	680
Available-to-Promise*	20		300		480	
Master Production Schedule (JIT MPS)			1000		1000	

Explosion into MRP

The determination of these lines will be covered later in this module.

Figure 5-1: Typical Master Schedule

STEPS IN DEVELOPING THE MASTER SCHEDULE

When developing a master schedule such as the one shown in Figure 5-1, consider the following steps:

1. Determine the category of manufacturing environment the product falls into—build-to-order, assemble-to-order, or build-to-stock.

2. Determine what the product families and categories will be and how their related bills of material will be structured.

3. Determine the planning horizon and time fences for the master schedule.

4. Calculate the lead times for customers' internal manufacturing, suppliers.

5. Establish guidelines for the implementation of capacity strategy developed in the manufacturing strategy. Supplier capacity must be part of this process.

6. Establish the policies and procedures that will guide such things as customer prioritization, definition of time fences, and allowances for changes.

Now let's look at each of these activities in more detail, as they relate to the various environments:

STEP 1 Determine the category of manufacturing environment the product falls into—build-to-order, assemble-to-order, or build-to-stock.

In an assemble-to-order environment, the MPS builds options made up of components and subassemblies; the final assembly schedule (FAS) is the final integration of the exact customer configuration. When you are building in this environment, you build to a certain level in the bill of material (BOM), then assemble to specific customer configuration. A planning BOM is used to accomplish this; it will be discussed later in this module.

In the build-to-order environment, the MPS builds only to customer orders. In this environment, the stocking point is raw material. The MPS is driven from that point by a customer order. Lead-times in a build-to-order environment tend to be greater than in an assemble-to-order environment.

In a build-to-stock environment, the MPS builds primarily to forecast.

STEP 2 Determine what product families will be and how their relationship to BOMs will be structured.

A product family is a category of products that have similar characteristics. Product families are established in the production planning process and then integrated into the master scheduling process.

Grouping of products into families reduces the detail in the master schedule. It also facilitates the scheduling at the narrowest part of the BOM. The figure below shows this:

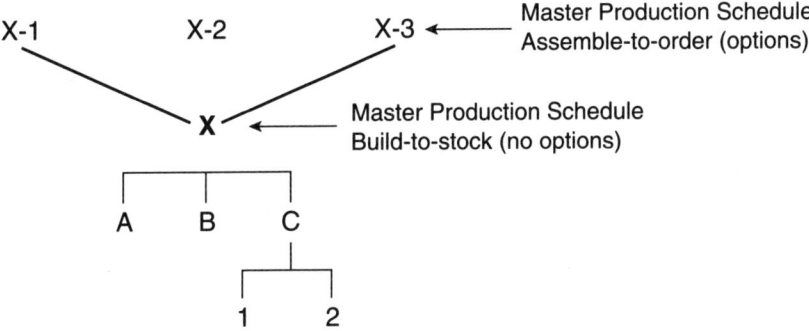

Figure 5-2: Product X Categories

The development of the master schedule includes designing the interface between the Production Plan and the Master Schedule.

STEP 3 Determine the planning horizon and time fences for the master schedule.

The planning horizon is the period of time over which a company will project its plans into the future. The planning horizon for the business plan, production plan, and manufacturing strategies are from two to five years into the future.

In the master schedule the planning period will span a horizon of 12 to 18 months. As a minimum, this planning horizon must be as long as the cumulative lead time, so all parts in the BOMs can be planned and scheduled. However, most companies take into consideration the time it takes to make changes; so they buffer their lead time with "safety lead time." It is also recommended that additional time be considered at the lower levels to purchase parts in the BOM, for the suppliers to react to the changes.

STEPS IN DEVELOPING THE MASTER SCHEDULE (continued)

The master scheduling planning horizon is further defined by the use of time fences. These time fences define the parameters in which changes to customer orders can be made, as well as changes to capacity. Time fences are described as demand time fences, planning time fences, and capacity planning time fences.

The demand time fence covers a period of time in which—even if you wish to make a change—it would be very costly in terms of time and money. This period is based on estimates of how long it takes to make changes in customer orders, the forecast, manufacturing and supplier lead times.

It is very important to determine what caused the change and the related costs (premiums, expediting, transportation, etc.). If customers cause the change they should pay; if suppliers cause the change they should pay; and if the company caused the change they should pay. Not recouping this cost of change from customers and suppliers is one of the major contributors to the "hidden cost of manufacturing" and the subsequent erosion of profit margins.

Changes within the demand time fences must be authorized by an appropriate level within the management ranks and include accounting, so the cost of the change can be properly accounted for. Changes may be made if there is available inventory and/or capacity, or a major competitive advantage can be achieved.

Beyond the demand time fence, the demand is made up of a combination of customer orders and forecasts. This period of time represents the rest of the planning time fence.

The planning time fence is made up of firm planned orders, which are orders that can be frozen in quantity and time. The computer software must be overridden manually to make changes.

Some companies will also designate a capacity planning time fence. This is used for longer-term capacity planning only. Normally, no master production schedule explosions are scheduled in this time period.

A summary of these time fences is shown in Figure 5-3.

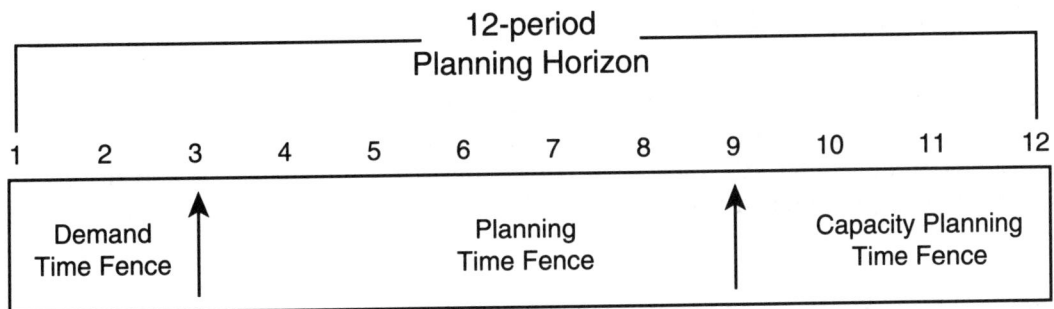

Figure 5-3

| STEP 4 | Calculate the lead times for customers, internal manufacturing, and suppliers. |

The figure below shows how three major types of lead time impact the actual physical flow of goods:

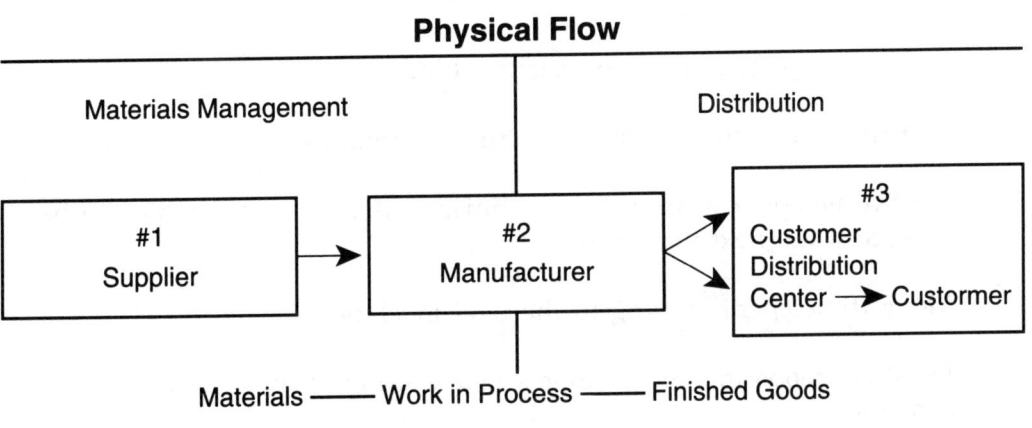

The three major types of lead time are customer lead time (customer orders), manufacturing lead time (work orders), and supplier lead time (purchase orders).

STEPS IN DEVELOPING THE MASTER SCHEDULE (continued)

Customer Lead Time

The customer lead time begins with order entry—either directly into the master schedule, or first through an order entry module that checks for order correctness, credit status, etc., and then into the master schedule. It ends when the order ships.

Manufacturing Lead Time

The customer orders, once entered into the master schedule, create work orders or purchase orders via the MRP system.

The time from the work order release until the order is complete makes up manufacturing lead time. This lead time varies based on the type of manufacturing. The major components of lead time are:

- Queue (the time the inventory is sitting on the shop floor waiting to be worked on)

- Setup (time spent preparing the machine)

- Run time (time the machine is actually running)

- Wait (time spent waiting for the finished item at one machine to be moved to the next machine)

- Move (time spent moving to the next machine)

- Finished goods inventory (time spent waiting to move to the end customer)

Supplier Lead Time

Supplier lead time includes the time to get a purchase requisition, release it as a purchase order to the supplier, and receive it into the warehouse or directly to the production floor.

Reconciling the Physical Flow with the Information Flow

Reconciling the information flow (from MPS through MRP and on to the suppliers) with the physical flow of the parts from suppliers into manufacturing and then on to the customers is one of the major challenges in companies today.

In many cases, products can actually be built faster than orders can be entered and processed through the manufacturing and purchasing information systems. In many companies meeting time-to-market objectives, information systems bottlenecks have taken the place of manufacturing (machine) bottlenecks.

This situation worsens when unexpected changes occur, especially customer changes. Marketing people, financial people and particularly executives have little appreciation for the time the entire process takes. It takes time to analyze and make corrections or changes, not just to the customer order, but all the way through manufacturing and the affected suppliers.

Additional time and considerable talent in negotiating must be used with the suppliers and the operations people to make changes.

This situation causes a large number of part shortages and late deliveries, both from suppliers and to customers. In addition, costs such as premiums and expedited charges are incurred, which seldom get passed on to the customer.

The answer to this problem is threefold:

1. Account management needs to point out to the customers the cost of the changes they are asking for. (Especially the next time cost reductions are being negotiated.)

2. Manufacturing software needs to be significantly improved to allow for instantaneous updates and access to all the information.

3. Accounting systems need to track the cost of these customer changes so a determination can be made in terms of who pays for the changes: the suppliers, your company, or the customer. The answer should revolve around who caused or initiated the change and why it was necessary.

STEPS IN DEVELOPING THE MASTER SCHEDULE (continued)

STEP 5 — Establish guidelines for the implementation of the capacity strategy developed in the production planning portion of the manufacturing strategy setting. Supplier capacity must be a part of this process.

Rough-cut capacity planning (RCCP), also known as resource requirement planning, is the process of converting the MPS into capacity needs for key resources: people, equipment, facilities, supplier's capabilities, and money required to fund acquisitions.

The purpose of RCCP is to assist the master scheduler in establishing a feasible master production schedule.

In order to complete the process of testing the master production schedule, any bottleneck work centers must be identified. A bottleneck work center is one in which the smallest number of units can be completed in one or multiple shifts within a 24-hour period.

Picture a manufacturing facility as a funnel. The *capacity* is the rate at which the work is withdrawn from the bottom of the funnel. The *load* is the volume of the work in the funnel. Figure 5-4 on page 103 illustrates this concept.

As we have seen in this module, the Master Product Schedule must be realistic. This means that before you commit orders, the MPS must be tested within the capacity constraints of the production facility. In this context, capacity is defined in terms of output per machine or person per shift. Without sufficient capacity, customer delivery dates may be missed.

The bill of capacity helps the MPS in testing for capacity. A bill of resources is a list of required capacity and key resources needed to produce one unit of a typical product. In rough-cut capacity planning, these bills of resources are used to calculate the approximate capacity requirements of the MPS.

Lead-time offsets are included in the bill of resources. Lead-time offset enables you to determine the impact of the potential customer due date when you are scheduling the shop floor and the suppliers. Lead-time and lead-time offset enable the time-phasing process to take place.

The bill of capacity shows the labor and machine time required to produce a typical unit of product. When you multiply the capacity required to produce the typical unit times the units required by the MPS, you have the total units per period.

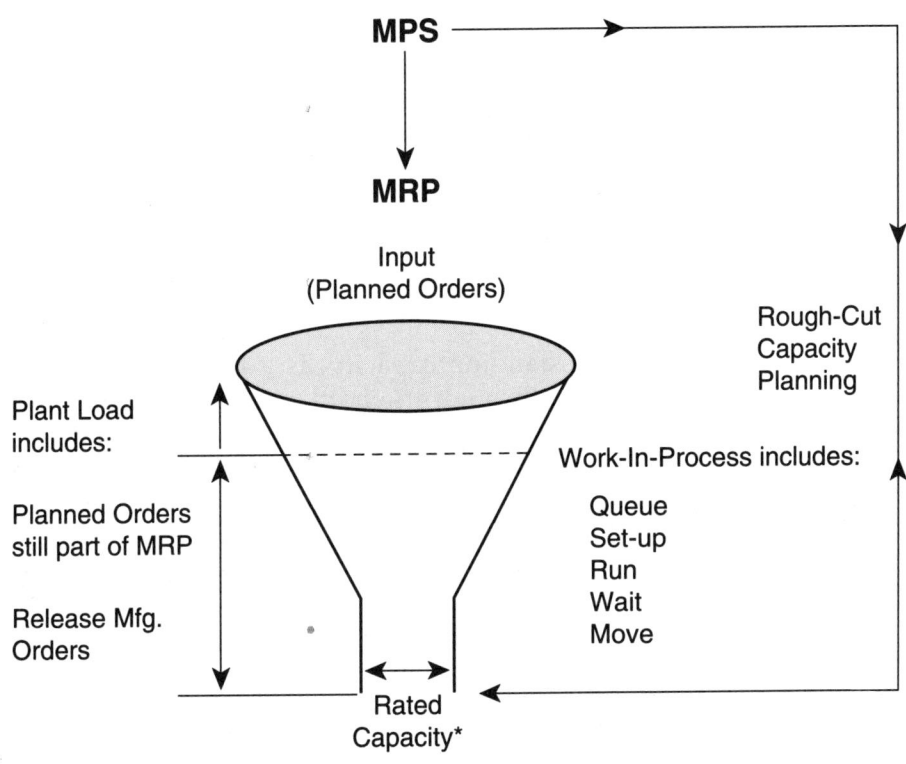

Figure 5-4 Capacity vs. Load

This process produces a report called the rough-cut capacity plan, which shows any shortfalls of capacity of critical resources.

If there are no imbalances between the load of the projected sales/revenue and the available capacity, the plan is ready for execution.

However, if imbalances in the form of shortages of critical resources do occur in one or more of the master schedules, the shortages must be rolled back up and adjustments made to reduce the production plan, revenue/sales plan, and projected inventory levels or increase resources, such as the acquisition of more capital equipment, people, material and—most importantly—the funding required to purchase these items.

Failure to ensure that the checks and balances between resource planning, production planning, master scheduling, and rough-cut capacity planning can result in missed shipments, low customer satisfaction, and higher inventories.

STEPS IN DEVELOPING THE MASTER SCHEDULE (continued)

Failure to balance out the high-level production and resource plans will cause problems throughout the rest of the planning and execution process. The objectives of medium-term plans contained in the master schedules and the short-term plans contained in the material requirement plans will not be achieved.

Rated Capacity

Rated capacity (also known as standing capacity) is a formula for calculating the number of units that can go through the bottleneck work center. Traditionally, capacity is calculated from such data as planned hours, efficiency, and utilization. Refer to Figure 5-4 on page 103 to see where rated capacity fits in the (MPS?) process. Other terms used in capacity planning are "theoretical capacity" and "demonstrated capacity." Theoretical capacity assumes that machines and people are used 100% of the time, and that they are 100% efficient. In practice theoretical capacity is seldom, if ever, achieved. Demonstrated capacity represents how much capacity was used in the past.

Rated Capacity Formula

The following is a rated capacity formula that may be modified to include other industry-specific factors such as the machine jam factor as in the semiconductor industry. You should identify any conditions that impact the capacity of unit production.

> Rated Capacity = Machine and/or people
> × Hours per shift
> × Shifts per day
> × Efficiency
> × Utilization*
> × Days per week, month, etc.
> = Standard Hours
> × Units per hour
> = Units per day, week, month

* Reasons for not utilizing equipment/machines during an 8-hour shift might be:

- Planned maintenance
- Unplanned maintenance
- Setup
- Absenteeism
- Meetings
- Material shortages
- Lack of customer orders
- Material defects

The final two lines are the Projected Available Balance (PAB) and the Available-to-Promise (ATP) line.

PAB represents the inventory balance projected into the future. The formula for the Projected Available Balance is:

Before the Demand Time Fence:
   Prior period PAB + MPS − customer orders = PAB

After the Demand Time Fence:
   Prior period + MPS − Forecast or customer order (whichever is greater) = PAB

Available-to-Promise represents the unsold capacity, the capacity to produce units to be sold to customers. This calculation can be period-by-period or it can be stated as a cumulative amount.

ATP is the uncommitted inventory balance in the first period and is normally calculated for each period in which an MPS receipt is scheduled. In the first period ATP includes on-hand inventory less customer orders. The formula for ATP is:

   Beginning Inventory (in 1st period only) + MPS − the sum
      of the customer orders before the next MPS

STEPS IN DEVELOPING THE MASTER SCHEDULE (continued)

Now finish the exercise below.

You will complete Figure 5-5 with the results of calculations in the exercises below.

Jade, Inc.
Master Schedule—Build-to-Stock

Item: 1645ASTER
Description: Pen

Run Date: 09-13-XX
Planning Horizon: 6
④ Demand Time Fence: 3

	Period		1	2	3	4	5	6
⑤	Forecast		360	420	340	340	240	280
③	Customer Orders		380	400	300	400	120	400
①	Projected Available Balance (Inventory)	800	420					
⑥	Available-to-Promise		20					
②	Master Production Schedule				1000		1000	

▼ ▼
Explosion into MRP

Figure 5-5: Typical Master Production Schedule

Use the following formulas:

▶ Projected Available Balance ① = prior period inventory + MPS ② − Customer Orders ③

▶ Projected Available Balance (after the Demand Time Fence ④) = prior period inventory + MPS − the greater of either Customer Orders or Forecast ⑤

▶ Available to Promise ⑥ = First Period Beginning Inventory + MPS − the total of Customer Orders until the next MPS.

EXERCISE 6

Projected Available Balance (PAB)

The chart below shows an example of the Projected Available Balance (PAB) formula. This is a non-cumulative PAB. Answers for this exercise follow on page 112.

Before Demand Time Fence

Period	Prior Period PAB	+ MPS or On-hand	– Customer Order	= PAB
1	800	+0	minus 380	= 420
2	420	+0	minus 400	= 20
3	20	+1000	minus 300	= 720

1. Using the information provided above, complete the following chart for periods 5–6.

After Demand Time Fence

Period	Prior Period PAB	+ MPS or On-hand	– Forecast or Customer Order (whichever is greater)	= PAB
4	720	+ 0	– 400	= 320
5				
6				

2. Now complete the following chart for Available-to-Promise (ATP)

Period	Beginning Inventory (first period only)	+ MPS	– Total of customer orders before the next MPS	Non-cumulative ATP	Cumulative ATP*
1					
3					
5					

*Cumulative ATP is calculated by adding the non-cumulative ATP answer in Period 1 to the subsequent non-cumulative ATPs in Periods 3 and 5.

EXERCISE 6 (continued)

3. Write the formula for PAB and then complete the master schedule below using the following information for Product Standard Jade Ink Pen:

   Lead-time: 1
   On hand: 800
   Lot size: 500
   Safety stock: 100
   Demand time fence: 2
   Planning time fence: 4

Periods		1	2	3	4
Forecast		400	400	400	400
PAB	800				
MPS			500		500

4. Given: Build-to-Order (Non-cumulative)

   Lead-time: 1
   On hand: 0
   Lot size: 500
   Safety stock: 0
   Demand time fence: 2
   Planning time fence: 4

Periods		1	2	3	4
Forecast		400	400	400	400
Orders			500		350
PAB	500				
ATP					
MPS		500	500		500

   From the information above, write the formula for PAB and ATP, then complete the table.

5. In this exercise you will determine capacity and identify the bottleneck work center for a job shop.

Using the following formula, recalculate the rated capacity (work center capacity hours) for work centers 700, 750, and 400.

Using the same formula, calculate rated capacity for work centers 020, 500, and 550.

> **Formula for Determining Rated Capacity**
>
> (shifts per day) × (machines or work stations)
> × (hours per shift) × (utilization) × (efficiency)
> = standard hours per day per work center capacity

Assumptions:

- 8 working hours, 1 shift

WC No.	WC Descrip.	# of Machines	Machine Utilization	Efficiency	① WC Cap. in Hrs per Day	② UPHs Units per Hours	③ Units per Day	④ Units/Mo. (20-day Mo.)
700	Dip Insertion	2	.90	.90	12.96	5		
750	Axiel Insertion	4	.90	.85	24.48	7		
400	Cut & Clinch	6	.85	1.10	44.88	5		
020	Wave Solder	1	.90	.90		5		
500	ATE	3	.80	1.05		6		
550	Functional Test	2	.90	1.00		4		

(Explanation of work to be performed is continued on page 100.)

EXERCISE 6 (continued)

Column	What to do
②	This information has been provided for you, based on engineering estimates and history.
③	Multiply column 1 × column 2.
④	Multiply column 3 × 20 work days.

If the MPS calls for shipping 1200 units:

6. Identify the bottleneck work center(s), if any. _____

7. Suggest how you would increase the bottleneck work center's capacity.

Short-Term: (next 30 days)

_____

_____

_____

Medium-Term: (30–360 days)

_____

_____

_____

Long-Term: (1–5 years)

_____

_____

_____

8. List the six steps in developing the master schedule.

_____

_____

_____

_____

_____

_____

EXERCISE 6 ANSWERS

1. Now complete the following chart for periods 5-6.

   After Demand Time Fence

Period	Prior Period PAB	+ MPS or On-hand	− Forecast or Customer Order (whichever is greater)	= PAB
4	720	+ 0	− 400	= 320
5	320	+1000	− 240	= 1080
6	1080	+0	− 400	= 680

2. Now complete the following chart for Available-to-Promise (ATP)

Period	Beginning Inventory (first period only)	+ MPS	− Total of customer orders before the next MPS	Non-cumulative ATP	Cumulative ATP
1	800	+0	−780 (380 + 400)	= 20	20
3	0	+1000	−700 (300 + 400)	= 300	320
5	0	+1000	−520 (120 + 400)	= 480	800

3. **Required.** Write the formula for PAB and then complete the master schedule below.

   Given

   Product Standard Jade Ink Pen

   Lead-time: 1
   On hand: 800
   Lot size: 500

   Safety stock: 100
   Demand time fence: 2
   Planning time fence: 4

Periods		1	2	3	4
Forecast		400	400	400	400
PAB	800	400	500	100	200
MPS			500		500

$$\text{PAB} = \frac{\text{Prior period PAB or}}{\text{on-hand balance}} + \text{MPS} - \text{Customer orders (Forecast)}$$

PAB_1	=	800	+	0	−	400	=	400
PAB_2	=	400	+	500	−	400	=	500
PAB_3	=	500	+	0	−	400	=	100
PAB_4	=	100	+	500	−	400	=	200

4. **Given**

   Lead-time: 1   Safety stock: 0
   On hand: 0   Demand time fence: 2
   Lot size: 500   Planning time fence: 4

Periods		1	2	3	4
Forecast		400	400	400	400
Orders			500		350
PAB	500	1000	1000	600	700
ATP		1000	0		150
MPS		500	500		500

PAB (prior)	=	Prior PAB or on-hand	+	MPS	−	Orders		
PAB_1	=			500	+ 500	− 0	=	1000
PAB_2	=			1000	+ 500	− 500	=	1000

PAB (after)	=	Prior PAB	+	MPS	−	Greater value of customer orders or forecast		
PAB_3	=			1000	+ 0	− 400	=	600
PAB_4	=			600	+ 500	− 400	=	700

EXERCISE 6 ANSWERS (continued)

Available-to-promise = On-hand balance (1st period only) + MPS − Sum of customer orders before next MPS

ATP1 = 500 + 500 − 0 = 1000

ATP2 = — + 500 − 500 = 0

ATP4 = — + 500 − 350 = 150

5.

WC No.	WC Descrip.	# of Machines	Machine Utilization	Efficiency	① WC Cap. in Hrs per Day	② UPHs Units per Hours	③ Units per Day	④ Units/Mo. (20-day Mo.)
700	Dip Insertion	2	.90	.90	12.96	5	64.80	1296
750	Axiel Insertion	4	.90	.85	24.48	7	171.36	3427
400	Cut & Clinch	6	.85	1.10	44.88	5	224.4	4488
020	Wave Solder	1	.90	.90	6.48	5	32.4	648
500	ATE	3	.80	1.05	20.16	6	120.9	2419
550	Functional Test	2	.90	1.00	14.4	4	57.6	1152

6. According to the data, the bottleneck work centers would appear to be: *020* and *550*.

7. Suggestions for increasing capacity:

   Short-Term
   - Add overtime hours
   - Subcontract
   - Continuously improve process

Medium-Term
- Improve machine utilization and efficiency
- Add shifts
- Subcontract—if the whole line was subcontracted
- Improve units per hour (UPH)
- Add people
- Continuously improve the process

Long-Term
- Add capital equipment
- Add facilities
- Develop long-term supplier relationship
- Use new technologies

8. List the six steps in developing the master schedule.

   a. Determine the category of manufacturing environment the product falls into—engineer-to-order, build-to-order, assemble-to-order, or build-to-stock.

   b. Determine what the product families and categories will be and how their related bills of material will be structured.

   c. Determine the planning horizon and time fences for the master schedule.

   d. Calculate the lead time for internal manufacturing from your suppliers and you, as well as the customers' expectation of your product's availability.

   e. Establish guidelines for the capacity strategy developed in the manufacturing strategy setting process. Supplier capacity must be part of these guidelines.

   f. Establish the policies and procedures that will guide such things as customer prioritization, definition of time fences, and allowances for changes.

The JIT Forecasting and Master Scheduling model and related tools which have been covered in this book are intended to be only a guide. You may use some or all of these in the development of your model. Everything is in degrees.

Assessment

JIT FORECASTING AND MASTER SCHEDULING

JIT FORECASTING AND MASTER SCHEDULING

A FIFTY-MINUTE™ BOOK

The objectives of this book are:

1. to explain the techniques and advantages of long-term planning.

2. to present a just-in-time forecasting model.

3. to explain how to use forecasting tools.

Disclaimer:
These assessments were written to test the reader on the content of the book. They were not developed by a professional test writer. The publisher and author shall have neither liability nor responsibility to any person with respect to any loss or damage caused or alleged to be caused directly or indirectly by the assessment contained herein.

OBJECTIVE ASSESSMENT FOR JIT FORECASTING AND MASTER SCHEDULING

Select the best response.

1. If a company cannot predict accurately its customer demand, it will probably
   A. carry too much inventory.
   B. pay unnecessary manufacturing costs.
   C. spend money too early.
   D. all of the above.
   E. none of the above.

2. Today's competitive advantage goes to companies that
   A. have learned to reduce costs.
   B. are best at managing change.
   C. keep employees longest.
   D. produce goods most quickly.

3. A forecasting and master scheduling model must be
   A. driven by customer demands.
   B. part of an integrated planning system.
   C. a way to predict sales.
   D. driven by a marketing strategy.

4. When product variety increases, product volume
   A. increases.
   B. decreases.

5. The highest profit margin per unit is in a manufacturing environment of
   A. engineered-to-order goods.
   B. built-to-order goods.
   C. assembled-to-order goods.
   D. built-to-stock goods.

6. To set inventory levels, you must consider both customer satisfaction and expected
   A. quality of goods.
   B. forecast error.
   C. variation in resources.
   D. planning errors.

OBJECTIVE ASSESSMENT (continued)

7. Realistic production rates must be based on
    A. complete resource plans.
    B. data on resource availability.
    C. customer interest in the product.
    D. all of the above.
    E. A and B.

8. *Tracking* is a capacity strategy that plans for capacity
    A. well in advance of anticipated sales.
    B. only when customer demand is present.
    C. in relation to sales projections.
    D. only when inventory is low.

9. To balance conflicting goals of departments, such as sales, finance, and engineering, key components must have
    A. willingness to change.
    B. adequate time to change.
    C. both of the above.

10. Raw material is *least* likely to be held in inventory for
    A. engineered-to-order goods.
    B. built-to-order goods.
    C. assembled-to-order goods.
    D. built-to-stock goods.

11. Just-in-Time forecasting attempts to replace inventory with
    A. investments.
    B. information.
    C. income.
    D. increased revenue.

12. A forecast error is the difference between what you
    A. planned to sell and what you manufactured.
    B. sold and what your competitor sold.
    C. thought you could sell and what you sold.
    D. manufactured and what was defective.

13. Quantitative forecasting tools are
    A. graphic methods.
    B. a panel of experts.
    C. trend projections.
    D. arithmetic average.
    E. A, C and D.

14. Once you have established a forecasting model, it should not be changed.
    A. True
    B. False

15. A moving average forecasting tool is
    A. a new period plus prior periods divided by number of periods.
    B. same as A but the oldest period is dropped.
    C. when data is weighted.
    D. when data is weighted and the newest data counts most.

16. Full response forecasting requires that there be
    A. no variation in sales from year to year.
    B. a wide variation in sales from year to year.

17. Extrinsic forecasting indicators
    A. presume a constant relationship between two factors.
    B. are more useful for smaller product lines.
    C. can come from external or internal business sources.
    D. all of the above.
    E. A and C.

18. The standard deviation of the forecast error can determine the inventory needed to meet a probable shipping time.
    A. True
    B. False

19. The 80/20 rule is that
    A. *80%* of a population is a predictor of 100% of the effect.
    B. *20%* of a population is a predictor of 100% of the effect.
    C. a *small* percentage of a group has the greatest influence.
    D. a *large* percentage of a group has the greatest influence.

20. The formula for exponential smoothing is
    A. New forecast = old forecast + [$\alpha \times$ (actual demand − old forecast)].
    B. New forecast = old forecast + [$\alpha \times$ (actual demand + old forecast)].

21. In a build-to order-environment
    A. the stocking point is raw material.
    B. the Master Production Schedule is driven by customer orders.
    C. subassemblies are not built before customer orders arrive.
    D. all of the above.
    E. A and B.

OBJECTIVE ASSESSMENT (continued)

22. If suppliers or customers require changes to the master schedule, the company should absorb the cost of those changes.
    A. True
    B. False

23. If shortages of critical resources occur,
    A. production, sales and inventory levels must be adjusted.
    B. equipment, staff and materials must be provided as needed.
    C. necessary funding must be provided.
    D. all of the above.
    E. B and C.

24. To calculate the number of units that can be produced, use the
    A. rough-cut capacity plan.
    B. rated capacity formula.
    C. projected available balance formula.
    D. moving average technique.

25. Although JIT forecasting and master scheduling may seem to be contradictory, actually they are complementary because
    A. precise forecasting tools can be used.
    B. long term planning can enhance JIT forecasting.
    C. a tested model for forecasting is possible.
    D. all of the above.

Qualitative Objectives for *JIT Forecasting and Master Scheduling*

To explain the techniques and advantages of long term planning

Questions 1, 2, 3, 4, 5, 22, 23, 25

To present a just-in-time forecasting model

Questions 6, 7, 8, 9, 10, 11, 12, 14, 21

To explain how to use forecasting tools

Questions 13, 15, 16, 17, 18, 19, 20, 24

ANSWER KEY

1. D
2. B
3. B
4. B
5. A
6. B
7. D
8. C
9. C
10. A
11. B
12. C
13. E
14. B
15. B
16. A
17. E
18. A
19. C
20. A
21. E
22. B
23. D
24. B
25. D

NOTES

NOTES

NOTES

NOW AVAILABLE FROM CRISP PUBLICATIONS

Books • Videos • CD Roms • Computer-Based Training Products

If you enjoyed this book, we have great news for you. There are over 200 books available in the *50-Minute*™ Series. To request a free full-line catalog, contact your local distributor or Crisp Publications, Inc., 1200 Hamilton Court, Menlo Park, CA 94025. Our toll-free number is 800-442-7477.

Subject Areas Include:

Management
Human Resources
Communication Skills
Personal Development
Marketing/Sales
Organizational Development
Customer Service/Quality
Computer Skills
Small Business and Entrepreneurship
Adult Literacy and Learning
Life Planning and Retirement

CRISP WORLDWIDE DISTRIBUTION

English language books are distributed worldwide. Major international distributors include:

ASIA/PACIFIC

Australia/New Zealand: In Learning, PO Box 1051, Springwood QLD, Brisbane, Australia 4127   Tel: 61-7-3-841-2286, Facsimile: 61-7-3-841-1580
ATTN: Messrs. Gordon

Singapore: 85, Genting Lane, Guan Hua Warehouse Bldng #05-01, Singapore 349569   Tel: 65-749-3389, Facsimile: 65-749-1129
ATTN: Evelyn Lee

Japan: Phoenix Associates Co., LTD., Mizuho Bldng. 3-F, 2-12-2, Kami Osaki, Shinagawa-Ku, Tokyo 141   Tel: 81-33-443-7231, Facsimile: 81-33-443-7640
ATTN: Mr. Peter Owans

CANADA

Reid Publishing, Ltd., Box 69559-109 Thomas Street, Oakville, Ontario Canada L6J 7R4.   Tel: (905) 842-4428, Facsimile: (905) 842-9327
ATTN: Mr. Stanley Reid

Trade Book Stores: *Raincoast Books,* 8680 Cambie Street, Vancouver, B.C., V6P 6M9   Tel: (604) 323-7100, Facsimile: (604) 323-2600
ATTN: Order Desk

EUROPEAN UNION

England: *Flex Training,* Ltd. 9-15 Hitchin Street, Baldock, Hertfordshire, SG7 6A, England   Tel: 44-1-46-289-6000, Facsimile: 44-1-46-289-2417
ATTN: Mr. David Willetts

INDIA

Multi-Media HRD, Pvt., Ltd., National House, Tulloch Road, Appolo Bunder, Bombay, India 400-039   Tel: 91-22-204-2281, Facsimile: 91-22-283-6478
ATTN: Messrs. Aggarwal

SOUTH AMERICA

Mexico: *Grupo Editorial Iberoamerica,* Nebraska 199, Col. Napoles, 03810 Mexico, D.F.   Tel: 525-523-0994, Facsimile: 525-543-1173
ATTN: Señor Nicholas Grepe

SOUTH AFRICA

Alternative Books, Unit A3 Micro Industrial Park, Hammer Avenue, Stridom Park, Randburg, 2194 South Africa   Tel: 27-11-792-7730, Facsimile: 27-11-792-7787
ATTN: Mr. Vernon de Haas